Contents

Our Experience of Colour

What we experience as colour is the interaction between light and darkness. In spiritual terms, "Light" was the first act of Creation and the beginning of separation between the things that might be possible and those that were made real. We are born into the light of the world and we die and are gathered into the Light of Spirit.

For most people, colour is a continuing experience, and this is true even for those who are born blind or who have lost their sight. From the time we wake to the time we go to sleep, colour is all around us—in nature, in the buildings in which we work and live, and in the clothes we wear. When we close our eyes and see inner images, like all other types of energy, the energy of the colours we see has an effect upon us.

We are beings of light. Portions of our own subtle energy field (or aura) store information as colour, which can be perceived clairvoyantly as fields of colour that fluctuate with changes in our physical, mental, emotional, and spiritual states. Colour has always been important in spiritual, psychic, and esoteric work because of the ways it can affect us.

You know more about colour than you believe you do. Your unconscious mind already knows about colour and selects the colours that express something about you and your inner state. For example, how many times have you taken a shirt out of your drawer, put it on, and thought, "Wrong colour for today!" and then replaced it with a shirt of another colour?

You might not have been able to analyze why that was, but you instinctively knew that the replacement colour was right because it "felt better."

By applying your knowledge of the effects of colour to every aspect of your life, you can empower yourself to:

- Choose the colours you wear for all occasions and know what they say about you

- Know what colours to use to decorate your environment for a particular effect

- Understand others through the colours they choose to wear

- Improve your health through application of coloured light, through awareness of colour and nutrition in foods, and by doing colour meditations

- Get more in touch with the subtle side of life and your spirituality

- Appreciate the full spectrum that life has to offer

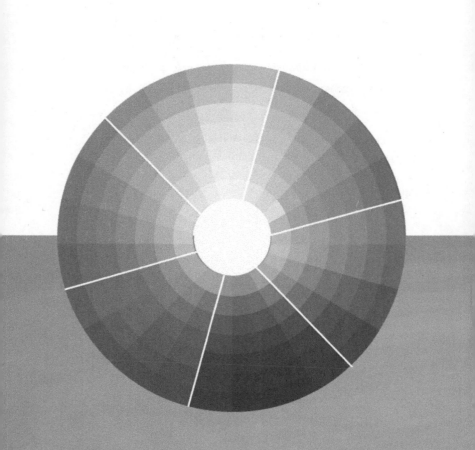

The Colour Spectrum

1

The symbolism and application of colours are vast. I have therefore addressed each colour individually and given an overview of its physical, emotional, and mental characteristics and meanings, as well as described its application in diet, decor, and fashion.

Describing a colour is difficult because we all perceive colours slightly differently. I have had more disagreements with people about what colour I am wearing than I can count! It is therefore useful to describe colours in reference to the living world, for example, sunflower yellow, forget-me-not blue, sky blue, pumpkin orange, fire-engine red, and so on.

I hope that this will set your mind working and inspire you to acknowledge how much you already understand about the nature of each colour. This will give you some insight into colour as well as give you a summary to refer to in the future.

Colour Basics

Colours are neither good nor bad. Each colour has particular properties relating to physical, emotional, mental, and spiritual states of being. Colours can be stimulating or depressing, constructive or destructive, attractive or repellent. They affect us more profoundly than we realize, a factor that becomes evident in the language we use to describe sensations, emotions, and situations.

Colour contains information. For instance, the colour series red-yellow-green is now so deeply embedded in our culture that its use is always read as stop-wait-go. Maps display colour schemes to make them easy to read and understand. Colour is used to draw attention to important information. It helps us to differentiate and remember data or facts, such as in the use of colour coding on wiring or pipes in industry, and it helps us to define identity, such as in flags and uniforms.

Guidelines for Understanding the Meanings of Colour

There are hot colours—red, yellow, and orange. There are cool colours—blue, green, and violet. Bright or highly contrasting colours draw the eye more quickly and are easier to see than pastel or low-contrast colours. They also define moods.

Colours indicate energy states that are either active and outgoing or receptive and inward turning. For example, both primary and secondary colours that are bright are perceived as being outgoing and active, as in fire-engine red or sunflower yellow. We all choose and use colours that are right for their purposes. Imagine having a candy-striped courtroom!

Use the following guidelines:

- In a combined colour, we perceive the more dominant colour as more influential. For example, in red-orange, red is the dominant colour.

- Whenever white or black is added to a bright colour, it progressively dilutes that colour until it is completely absorbed by the black or white, and it changes the colour's meaning accordingly.

- When white is added to a bright colour, the psychological impact of that colour becomes more innocent, ethereal, or insipid.

- When black is added to a bright colour, the psychological impact of that colour becomes more earthy, heavy, and repressed.

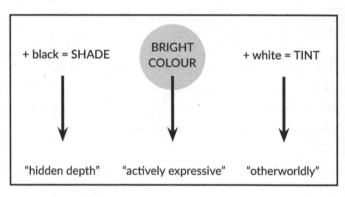

For Example: Red

Bright colour: Fire-engine red

Meaning: Extroversion, energy, sportiness, attention-seeking behavior, aggressiveness

Shade: Red + Black = Moroccan red

Meaning: Conservativeness, masculinity, sexiness, suppressed physical energy

Tint: Red + (a little) White = Hot pink

Meaning: Naughty innocence, teenage quality, assertiveness,
   energetic fun

Tint: Red + (a lot of) White = Baby pink

Meaning: Physical innocence, sweetness, softness,
   vulnerability

No matter how you use colours, the effect and the message they broadcast are the same whether applied to decor, fashion, advertising, or energy analysis and healing.

Once you think more deeply about colour, you can apply your knowledge to every area of life.

Chapter 17, "The Science of Colour," provides colour wheels and further explanations of how colours interact and combine.

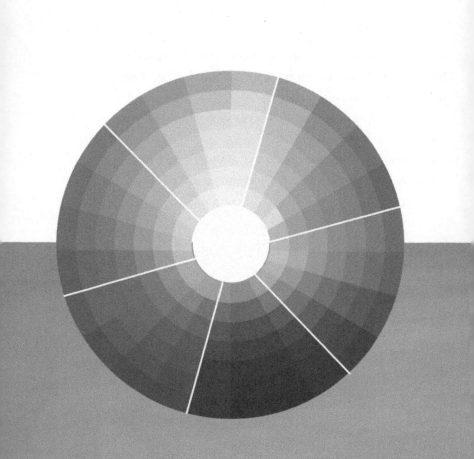

All
About
Red

2

Red appears as the densest colour of the spectrum and has the lowest vibrational frequency in the spectrum. Red is the colour that we associate with earthly matter, blood, and passion. It is a hot colour and is very stimulating, because even though the molecules vibrate slowly, they are densely packed, thus creating a lot of friction. This is why red catches our attention so rapidly and why it is so often used in advertising. It is so active that too much of it is overstimulating and irritating, so it needs to be used sparingly.

Red in the Aura

Red is naturally associated with the root chakra that governs survival on the physical plane and the fight-or-flight reflex regulated by the adrenal glands. Bright red in the aura signifies drug abuse or rage. Dark reds signify anger, rage, jealousy, or lust. Bright pinks signify irritation and frustration. Medium pinks signify a desire for physical activity, while pale pinks signify friendship, affection, and vulnerability.

Idiomatic Expressions

Idiomatic expressions using red colours include the following: red with rage, red rag to a bull, red-hot, red-hot mama, red light, red-light district, ruddy, scarlet woman.

Associations

Physical Associations

Element of fire, oxygenated blood, sexual excitement, physical heat as in fire, irritation, fevers, rashes, inflammation and swelling, stimulation through healthy exercise, health, vitality, vigor, virility, promoter of heat, stimulated nerves and blood and vitalized physical body, raw life force, hyperactivity

Emotional Associations

Anger, rage, temper, irritability, excitement, sexiness, action, passion, love of companionship, selfishness, need to have things now, present-oriented behaviour, generosity, assertiveness, self-aggrandizing behaviour, geniality, vigour, stubbornness, impulsiveness, physical approach to situations, creator of dramas, recklessness

Mental Associations

Stopping, paying attention, physical phase of mentality, love

Spiritual Associations

Mother Earth, death, fortune

Brights

Carmine: Anger

Scarlet: Lust

Crimson: Physicality

Shades

Blood red: Sensuality, uncontrolled passion

Brick red: Selfish motives, practical approach

Cordovan red: Coarse passion

Cloudy red: Greed and cruelty

Deep crimson: Materialism

Tints

"In the pink": Healthy

Hot pink: Innocent sexiness, active explorer, teenage energy, assertiveness

Baby pink: Physical innocence and reactivity, spiritual innocence, vulnerability

Rose pink: Selfless love, gentleness

Healing Applications

- Use red in small doses only, as pure red is hyperstimulating.

- Use for anemia and poor circulation. Red stimulates adrenaline and disperses tiredness, inertia, and coldness; red is expansive. Use red sparingly in cases of depression in combination with other colours.

- Use bright red for people who need get-up-and-go.

- For those with libido problems, use dark shades of red to stimulate a rush of blood to the lower regions.

- Use pink to gently stimulate metabolism or blood flow to an area.

- Colour breathing pink helps with weight loss.

Foods

Beetroot, radishes, black cherries, damsons, plums, spinach, cresses, currants, prunes, vegetables and fruit containing iron, red capsicums, chili peppers, cloves, red-ray-charged water

Decoration and Fashion

Use red sparingly as an accent colour to warm up a room. Use too much and the space will look like a brothel.

Dark reds are very masculine, sexy, and assertive and can be read as physically comfortable, warm, and stimulating. Red creates a sense of denseness and concentration, yet is very active. Use red to attract attention.

Red is a great accent colour for clothing. Wearing all red makes a very striking statement, and you have to be bold to carry this look. It is sexy, sassy, and aggressive. Wearing red can actually make you feel warm. For example, in winter wearing red socks makes your feet feel warm.

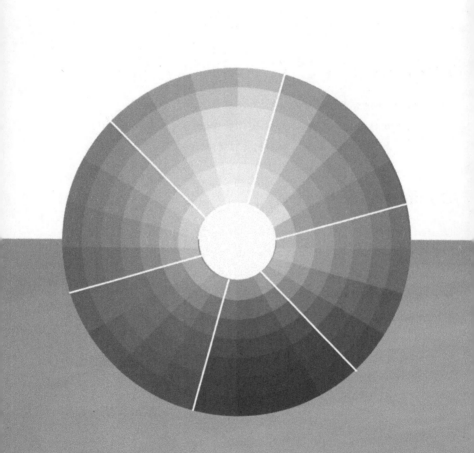

All About Orange

3

Combining red and yellow makes the range of orange colours. The symbolic keyword for red is "energy," and the keyword for yellow is "intellect." Orange is therefore energy that is focused by the mind. The dominance of the primary red or yellow in the mixture will determine how to interpret the symbolic meaning of the colour. For example, in red-orange there is more red than yellow; therefore, the *energy* of red will dominate the *logic* of yellow.

Orange is a warm, stimulating colour. It is less irritating than red but more physically active than yellow. We often find fast-food restaurants incorporating red, orange, and yellow in their advertising because orange promotes appetite, yellow helps in decision making, and red gets people in and out quickly.

Orange in the Aura

Orange naturally relates to the sacral chakra, which governs sexuality, gender identity, and social relationships. Whenever orange is found in the aura, it indicates that the person is doing something political or negotiating or learning to deal with people and to relate to them in a dynamic manner in social or business situations.

Idiomatic Expressions

There are no idiomatic expressions incorporating the colour orange that I know of.

Associations

Physical Associations

Stimulating, warm colour; appetite stimulant; vital, dynamic life force; tonic; stimulator of bodily functions; spleen, pancreas, lung, gall bladder, and liver strengthener; antispasmodic; aid to digestion and elimination

Emotional Associations

Political, manipulative, ambitious, motivating behaviour; feeling of well-being; promoter of action; pride of intellect; mastery by will; pride in mastery over others

Mental Associations

Negotiation skills, learning diplomacy and pride; stimulated mental functions

Spiritual Associations

Promoter of conscious control over physical functions

Brights

Bright orange: Energy, stimulation

Shades

Burnt orange: Pride, warmth, comfort, and motivation

Muddy orange: Judgment and manipulation

Brown orange: Playing safe in social contexts

Tints

Peach: Vulnerability, sensitivity

Apricot: Appetite promoter, sociability

Foods

Orange, tangerine, apricot, mango, peach, cantaloupe, carrot, butternut squash, pumpkin, yam, swedes (also known as rutabagas or by the marvelous British name, mangel-wurzel!), orange-charged water

Healing Applications

- Orange removes repressions and inhibitions, broadens the mind to new ideas, raises mental ability, brings understanding and tolerance, and raises motivation.

- Orange helps with muscle spasms or cramps.

- Use orange to increase vitality.

- Use orange to treat disorders of spleen and kidneys, gallbladder and liver.

- Use for paralysis and panic brought on by emotional problems.

- Use orange for breathing difficulties: helps treat asthma (along with the blue ray) and bronchitis.

- Orange stimulates elimination.

- Use orange to build stamina and bring heat to the body.

- Colour breathing orange stimulates a person into action and takes the person from stagnation and depression into motivation and directed energy.

Decoration and Fashion

Orange is a good colour to use in public areas, because its warmth promotes positive social interaction and feelings of comfort. It is good also for dining rooms and kitchens, and it helps "structure the fire" of an environment. Pale peach or apricot can be used in a playroom or nursery as a nurturing colour, as it promotes good relationships and is uplifting. Shades of orange warm up and give an earthy feeling to a room. Bright orange accents add zing to a room without being too irritating.

Use orange with blue, the opposite colour of orange.

Orange clothes or accents within clothing patterns send a bold, warm message in all shades. It is a good colour to use to create a more masculine feel, except in its paler tints.

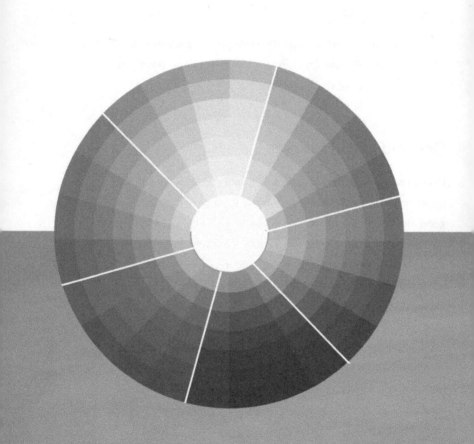

All
About
Yellow

4

Yellow is the colour that is associated with the mind. The function of the mind is dual, because the lower mind is involved in the logical thought process that organizes functioning within the world, but the higher mind connects us to the wisdom of the universe. Wisdom is the application of knowledge through love. Bright yellow is also the colour of joy, light, and laughter, or positive mental states. When mixed with white, yellows become less logical and more able to accept the emotional world, and they are also taken to indicate decreased mental power. When mixed with black, the yellows become more judgmental and prone to worry and negative thinking.

Yellow in the Aura

Yellow is naturally associated with the solar plexus chakra, which is related to making choices and making decisions. Whenever yellow is found in the aura, depending upon the shade, it signifies application of logic, learning, study, paperwork, complex legal matters, details, judgment of self or others, or worry.

Idiomatic Expressions

One idiomatic expression that uses the colour yellow is yellow-bellied (cowardly). Over the last century and a half, Americans have used yellow for remembrance, in tying a yellow ribbon around a tree when a loved one has gone away to fight in a war.

Associations

Physical Associations

Digestion, stomach, spleen, pancreas, gall bladder, liver, break-down and assimilation of nutrients, link to the functions of the left side of the brain (logic), purifier for the skin, paperwork, details

Emotional Associations

Joy, inspiration, optimism, cowardice, confusion caused by the mind overpowering the emotions

Mental Associations

Analysis, intellectualism, logic, eccentric thought, judgment, study and learning, discrimination, prejudice, absolutism, stubbornness, an attitude of "If I can't see it, I don't believe it," self-control

Spiritual Associations

Application of the higher mind and pure intellect or intellectual attainment. Sunflower yellow is associated with joy; golden yellow is associated with a high spiritual state of being.

Brights

Bright yellow: Joy, light, laughter, positive mental states

Shades

Ochre: Worry and self-doubt

Mustard: Judgment of self or others, out of negative thinking

Dark ochre: Paranoia, suspicion

Tints

Pale primrose: Great intellectual power

Lemon: Normal intellectual ability

Pale, creamy yellow: Limited intellect, wishy-washy mind

Metallic gold: Wisdom, consciousness of God, spiritual awakening, wealth, power, and status

Healing Applications

- Yellow is inspiring and intellectually elevating.

- Use yellow for nervous exhaustion, skin complaints, indigestion, constipation, flatulence, liver trouble, and diabetes.

- Yellow generates energy in the muscles and motor nerves and stimulates the flow of bile.

- Yellow has a positive effect on depression, inducing a positive mental vibration affecting the nervous system and physical vitality.

- Colour breathing yellow improves memory and concentration.

Foods

Banana, pineapple, lemon, grapefruit, sweet corn, butter, yellow squash, yellow capsicum, saffron, turmeric, garlic and onions, yellow solar-charged water.

Decoration and Fashion

Yellow has a stimulating effect on the mind. As a room colour, the more saturated tones can be uplifting and warming, bringing a sense of sunshine and joy into a room. Yellow used in kitchens or public rooms will stimulate discussion and help digestion. Use yellow in a study to promote intellectual activity. Yellow is a good brightening accent colour, but should not be used as a main wall colour in rooms required for relaxation such as bedrooms or bathrooms, due to its stimulating effect on the mind.

Bright yellow can be a difficult colour for many people to wear and is most often found as an accent colour within prints. Bright yellow can be very flattering on dark-skinned people, and shades of yellow can look good on people with dark or red hair and brown eyes. The paler tints of yellow are easier to wear and convey an image of organization and a positive outlook.

Gold jewelry is also considered to be an attribute of yellow, and it has always been a symbol of personal power, wealth, and status. It represents the masculine solar energy because it never fades, tarnishes, or changes, and it is hypoallergenic.

All
About
Green

5

Green is the colour of balance, harmony, and sympathy. It is the combination of yellow, at the hot end of the spectrum and blue at the cold end of the spectrum. As with every secondary colour, the dominant colour of the mixture governs which has the most influence.

Green in the Aura

Green is the natural colour of the heart chakra, so it governs empathy, connection to one's life purpose, and the seat of the soul. Green is the colour of nature and refreshment through the abundance of nature. When we do not trust, we are out of balance with the natural world and do not believe that we will get what we require. This creates feelings of jealousy, resentment, and envy, all appearing as green within the energy field.

Bright green indicates a positive, practical, generous outlook on life. Dark greens signify jealousy, envy, and lack of self-esteem as well as resentment. Pale greens are associated with new ventures of a practical nature.

Idiomatic Expressions

Idiomatic expressions that use the colour green include the following: green thumb, green fingers, green pastures, greenhorn, green (eco-friendly), green with envy.

Associations

Physical Associations

Controlling the heart, immunity; influencing blood-pressure; practicality; being busy and productive; versatility and capability for creative but practical activities, such as crafts or gardening

Emotional Associations

Nurturer, one who is adaptable, versatile, and practical; independence or dependence; trust or lack of trust; new ventures; sympathy, kindness, peacefulness, security; fear of being emotionally hurt, vulnerability; love of home and food; envy, insecurity

Mental Associations

Deceit, treachery, jealousy, trouble saying no and setting boundaries, the need to delegate responsibilities

Spiritual Associations

Renewal, new life, vitality residing in nature

Brights

Bright greens: Positive, practical, generous

Shades

Forest green: Emotional security over physical matters

Khaki green: Jealousy, deceit

Olive green: Insecurity and low self-esteem

Dark olive: Miserliness and selfishness

Tints

Pale blue-green: Charity, altruistic emotion

Leaf green: Confidence, enthusiasm for new projects

Pale green: State of being untried, fresh, calming

Foods

All green fruits and vegetables as well as herbs—these foods are high in mineral and fiber content and are very nourishing on a cellular level, and they help cleanse and oxygenate the system; green solar-charged water

Healing Applications

- Green balances blood pressure, helps with headaches, and helps oxygenate the body.

- Green restores harmony to the nervous system, counteracting worry and nervous complaints.

- Green helps counteract malignancies and boosts immunity.

- Colour breathe green to boost the immune system and balance vitality in the etheric system.

Decoration and Fashion

In Ireland, one superstition dictates that it is bad luck to decorate in green. This superstition stems from the belief that the colour green is dead, as opposed to the living green of nature.

My friend and editor, Sasha, tells me that green was once considered an extremely unlucky colour to use in the home and that children, in particular, would not thrive in a house with green decor. The fact is that when Victorian paint manufacturers discovered how to make a nice, bright green, it became a very popular colour, but, apparently, these early paints contained arsenic. Some small children like to lick paint and chew the tops of banisters, newel posts and so on, and when they did, they got sick and sometimes died. Before it was discovered that it was the arsenic that was causing the problem, it was just assumed that green inside the home was unlucky. Some people still believe this superstition and will not buy green clothes, cars, or household items.

Green is restful and relaxing to the nervous system. With a dominance of blue in the mixture, it is a good colour to use when decorating bedrooms and living rooms. With a dominance of yellow, it is good as an accent colour, bringing a springlike energy into the space. Of course, one can always use plants, foliage, and flowers to draw green energy into a place. Sometimes one can consider the yard or garden to be a room within a property.

In fashion, forest greens emit a sense of emotional security. These colours are conservative in nature. Yellow-greens give a message of practical application of resources along with vitality to a situation, and they engender an aura of capability and responsibility.

All
About
Blue

6

There are more variations of the colour blue than of any other colour. These variations come from three primary types of blue: indigo, sky blue, and turquoise. Indigo is the colour of the night sky, which is deep and approaches the violet ray. One can also find ultramarine and royal blue, sky blue, teal, and turquoise. All these blue colours can also be mixed with black and white. Blue is the highest vibrational frequency of the primary colours, which means that there is a great deal of space between the molecules, which vibrate quickly. Blue is a cool colour. In nature we see the sky and water as exhibiting varying shades of blue, and this colour affects our higher ideas as well as our emotions.

Blue in the Aura

Turquoise and sky blue are associated with the throat chakra, which is the center of self-expression. Indigo is associated with the third-eye chakra, which is the center of vision and clairvoyance. Blue in the aura is the colour of emotional sensitivity and represents the need to take control of a situation. It also indicates developing the ability to communicate, not only with words, but also through art and music:

Idiomatic Expressions

Idiomatic expressions using the colour blue include the following: blue with cold, feeling blue.

Associations

Physical Associations

Right side of the brain, endocrine system, central nervous system, organs of the throat and head, electromagnetism of the body. Blue contracts, restricts, and slows body functions. It is astringent, cooling, and antiseptic.

Emotional Associations

Calm, relaxation, depression, creativity

Mental Associations

Loyalty, sincerity

Spiritual Associations

Inspiration and devotion, idealism, pure religious feeling, mysticism

Brights

Clear indigo: Introspection, spiritual perspective, caution

Clear sky blue: Creativity, idealism, caution

Clear turquoise: Freedom of expression, energetic creativity, risk taking

Shades

Navy: Conservatism, coolness on the outside and emotionality on the inside, state of being withdrawn

Slate: Depression

Teal: Attention to emotional aspects of practical matters, such as pensions, wills, mortgages, and the like

Dark turquoise: Fear of taking risks

Tints

Pale sky blue: Unrealistic idealism, naive emotionality

Ice blue: Hardness and coldness

Pale indigo: Unrealistic spirituality

Pale turquoise: Fear of commitment

Baby blue: Innocent spirituality

Healing Applications

- The sky blue ray cools fevers, infections, and inflammations, itching, and headaches. Use sky blue for shock, insomnia, and overexcitement. It is antiseptic and antispasmodic. It helps raise consciousness to the level of spirit.

- The indigo ray is anesthetic and hypnotic, and it regener-
  ates the mind and soul. Use it for psychosis and phobia,
  mental disorders, and diseases of the eye and nose.

- The turquoise ray can stimulate the nervous system, release
  blockages, and free the mind from rigid patterns.

- Colour breathing blue helps balance the emotions and is
  good to use when you want to ease yourself into meditation.

Foods

Red or black grapes, blackberries, blueberries, blue plums, blue
solar-charged water

Decoration and Fashion

Variations of sky blue and indigo are sedating, cool, and relaxing.
Turquoise is slightly more stimulating. These colours give a feeling
of space. They are good choices for bedrooms or any room where
one goes to relax. Too much blue can be dull, so use warm accent
colours or white to create a contrast. Different blues add variety
and look great when used together.

The colour blue conveys a message of conservatism and self-
control. Navy is often used in uniforms, as this colour conveys a
message of authority.

All About Violet

7

Violet is the highest vibration of light. The rays of the colour violet are stimulating to the nervous system. Violet is the combination of blue and red, which implies the spirit world taking charge over the physical plane. Historically, violet was so expensive to create that only royalty used it in their clothing. Since the advent of chemical dyes, violets and purples have become available to the masses. Symbolically, this means that we all need to take heed of our spiritual selves and use them to guide our daily lives.

Violet in the Aura

Violet naturally relates to the crown chakra, which governs our relationship to sunlight. It also governs our waking and sleeping cycles and connects us to geomagnetic north. It is intimately connected with the parasympathetic nervous system, which exerts control over our unconscious survival activities. Violet concerns our subconscious mind, our spiritual condition, and our ability to transform. Violet in the aura indicates an area where transformation is taking place at a deep level. This shows that long- and deeply buried issues are rising to the surface and can no longer be ignored. Life and death are now immediate and serious issues that need to be looked at. The variations in colour can indicate mourning and grief, spiritual isolation, emotional loneliness, and an inability to connect to others. Sometimes this can indicate spiritual delusion. Violet is the colour that promotes intuition and spiritual understanding.

Idiomatic Expressions

Idiomatic expressions that use violet colours include the following: royal colour, purple passion, colour of mourning, purple patch

Associations

Physical Associations

Lack of circulation, coldness, anesthetic, sedation of the nervous system

Emotional Associations

Power and control, sensitivity, isolation, compulsions

Mental Associations

Transformation, obsession, rigid adherence to protocols, love of ritual and form

Spiritual Associations

Spirituality, high attainment, holy love, intuition, spiritual consciousness

Brights

Violet: Spiritual attention, power, transformation

Purple: Mourning

Amethyst: Control over the material world using spiritual principles, nervous energy

Shades

Plum: Grieving

Gray/Mauve: Shame

Tints

Lilac: Isolation, being a hermit

Pale wisteria: A state not of this world

Foods

Blueberries, black grapes, blackberries, loganberries, wine, violet solar-charged water

Healing Applications

- Violet is used for mental illness, nervous and cerebral diseases, neurosis, neuralgia, epilepsy and rheumatic complaints, and pain relief.

- Violet is useful for treating insomnia and for inducing hypnotic states. It has a nourishing effect on those who feel they are mentally "burnt out."

- Violet is cooling and can help with burns.

- Violet is also used for concussions, tumours, and kidney and bladder diseases. Blue-purple shrinks things, while red-purple balances polarities of the body.

Decoration and Fashion

Purple is too strong a colour to use for decorating a whole room. It has a powerful effect on the nervous system that can be either sedating or irritating, depending on how much red there is in the mixture. Purple is a good secondary colour, as it can be quite masculine and gives a feeling of opulence and power to a room.

In clothing, purple is a colour that people have strong feelings about: they either love it or hate it. It has hippy and new age connotations and is also popular among witches. Purple is a colour that exudes power.

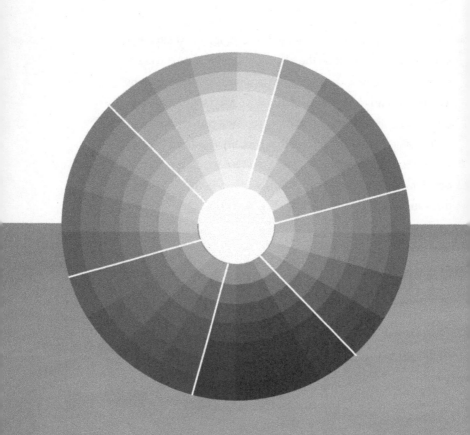

Black, White,
Gray, and
Brown

8

Black and white can be termed colours that are not colours! We have already seen that colour is everything that lies on the spectrum between black and white, but we can't leave these two out. Black and white make extremely powerful energetic statements. They are the polar opposites that can be said to represent good and evil. Do you see things in black and white or can you see the shades of gray?

Black

Black is comprised of all colours in an "unmanifest state," which means that they are there but they haven't yet been brought into being. If you think of being out somewhere in the countryside on a dark, moonless, and very cloudy night—one on which you cannot see the stars—you would not see anything other than blackness. This doesn't mean that the grass beneath your feet is anything other than green or the rocks are no longer gray, white, or brown; it just means that you cannot see the colours because without light, they are "unmanifest."

Black is said to be negative, receptive, and absorptive. Black represents a great mystery, where everything is hidden and all is potential, which is why it is such a compelling noncolour. It also represents the dark, where we cannot see clearly, and, therefore, it has been mistakenly labeled as evil and tempting.

White

White consists of all colours, which are "manifest" all at the same time. It is the ultimate luminescence. White is the colour of spirit and purity; it conveys a message of perfection, cleanliness, sterility, and pristine order. It gives off a cool, godlike, untouchable message. It is hard to challenge someone wearing white, as they take on an air of untouchable authority.

Grays

Gray is the colour of hiding, so those who wish to hide behind a "smoke screen" favor it. It conveys a nondescript, neutral image, through which no one can "see your hand of cards." Shades of gray also indicate subtleties behind issues. In the aura, gray relates to states of fear, exhaustion, lack of courage, depression, and negativity, whether it is present alongside another colour or combined with it. It can also indicate lack of imagination and meanness.

Browns

Combining all the primary colours forms a whole variety of different browns. Brown is the colour of security, practicality, and a down-to-earth approach. It is conservative, cautious, and slightly hidden. It can be seen as muddy, dirty, or indirect.

Browns symbolize the desire for gain and accumulation, on one hand, and miserliness and greed, on the other. If an aura reader sees brown in someone's aura, the client will be full of doubts, hedging his or her bets, or seeking the safe option.

Brown with white creates a variety of beiges and colours that are often associated with animal skins and furs. In some respects, these colours are very similar to gray in that they also convey safety, anonymity, and neutrality, but browns are warmer than grays.

Metallics

Gold, silver, bronze, brass, and copper colours can also be found in the aura, though these occasions are rare. As metals, they each relate to a different element and incorporate symbolic correspondences. They can be worn as jewellery and used in decor for specific energetic effects. They can also be used in healing.

- Gold relates to the solar ray, bringing warmth, luxury, and power to a situation.

- Silver relates to the lunar ray, bringing cool harmony to the emotions, along with receptivity. Silver also indicates versatility, but it can mean fickleness as well.

- Copper relates to the red ray, and stimulates hormone balance.

- Bronze relates to the orange ray, and though warming, it has a strong structuring element to it.

- Brass relates more to the yellow ray, and it can represent a brittle mentality.

Healing Applications

- Applying black and white or regulating the proportion of darkness and light in healing helps to regulate the inner clock for those who have insomnia or even hormonal difficulties.

- Dr. John Ott has proved that it is very important to have full-spectrum lightbulbs in a home or office. He has discovered that many physical and psychological complaints stem from restriction of exposure to the light spectrum by use of ordinary tungsten lightbulbs or by working under street lighting such as mercury or sodium-vapour lights. There are many who live in extreme northern or southern geographical areas who suffer from seasonal affective disorder (SAD), caused by inadequate exposure to sunlight. Seasonal affective disorder causes symptoms ranging from mild to severe depression. It can be treated by using exposure to an artificial full-spectrum light source for a minimum of thirty minutes a day.

- Brown is not often used in pure colour healing, or by applying solarized waters, or in colour breathing, because it is more effective to apply individual colours. You can see brown more frequently in actual medicine, such as in herbal tinctures, broths, stocks, and soups.

Foods

Gray foods are usually unhealthy and rotten—although some fish has grayish flesh when cooked.

Squid ink is black and full of minerals.

Milk is white and combines all the nutrients and immunity an infant requires in the first months of life—like white light! Fish flesh is frequently white. Many starchy foods are white or beige, such as bread, potatoes, rice, oats, barley, and so on.

Solarized water is a very useful tonic to the whole energy system. It can also carry subtle energies, so it is used to make vibrational remedies such as flower essences.

Brown foods are mostly found in grains and pulses and in animal protein (meat). This is interesting in that bread and meat have often been considered to be subsistence foods, and grains and pulses (beans) give a full vegetarian protein complement. Grains are considered to be "the staff of life," and they make breads and starch accompaniments to meals.

Brown colours in fruit and vegetables can indicate that the food is rotten or overripe.

Decoration and Fashion

In decor, black and white, either alone or together, make a bold and dramatic statement, and these colours can be seen as very masculine. Black is womblike and gothic, while white can be seen as sterile and pure. Either colour can be relaxing but also unrelenting. Together they suggest a rhythm that dances before the eyes, because the patterns these colours make become more important than the colours themselves.

Lighting and darkness can make or break the colour or patterns of a room. Lighting creates drama and is tremendously important from a practical standpoint. Whether one uses white light or coloured bulbs, the ambiance of a space is always affected.

Brown is earthy, relaxing, and warm—think of wood, for example. Although there are many shades of brown, and indeed many hues based on the dominant primary colour that is in the brown, if the whole room were brown, it would be textures rather than colour that would be seen as important. Brown is also a colour of conservative security. Using brown in decor intimates safety, so banks and certain types of shops use this colour to demonstrate that their organization is reliable and safe.

In fashion, the little black dress is the classic party number. It is very forgiving, as it can hide all one's lumps and bumps; it is mysterious and dressy; and it gives a sense of drama and power to the wearer. It is formal and anonymous. It does not go with all complexions, though, and it can make the wearer look washed out.

White is often used in uniforms, which can give an image of cleanliness, sterility, and authority. White is a summer colour that helps the wearer to stay cool because white reflects the light. White is dramatic. Bridal white is the symbol of virginity and purity, and, even in nonbridal situations, white can convey an air of innocence and spirituality. In some cultures it is the colour of mourning—to remind us that we all go back to an immaterial state—back to the Light of Spirit. White looks terrific on people with dark skin and/or hair.

Brown is a practical colour found in all aspects of the wardrobe, including pants, suits, coats, and everyday wear. It is rarely found in dressy clothing, except for furs and outfits with metallic colours such as bronze or copper. All tones of beige make a neutral and unthreatening statement, and beige looks good on people with blond or red hair.

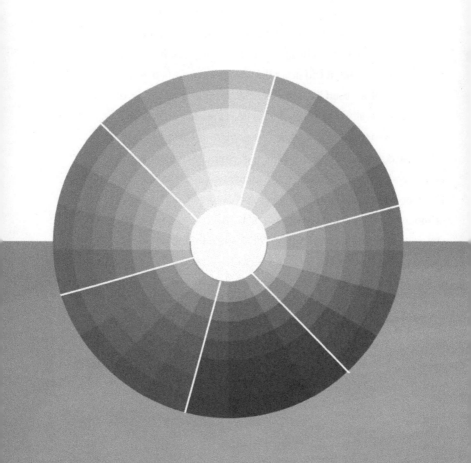

Colour and the Aura

9

We live in a world that includes a huge spectrum of energetic forces that help us to maintain our existence. Our physical body is biochemical in nature, so it requires food in the form of mineral, vegetable, and animal products to survive. All these substances have colour and exhibit properties that relate to the nature of that colour. Many native cultures that are in harmony with the Earth understand the relationships of shape and colour and the effect upon the human body in their healing traditions. In this book, we look at both the physical and the psychological effects of colours.

The field of energy that surrounds and sustains each individual is called an aura. This field has electromagnetic properties. It receives information from the outer environment at all wavelengths, it stores information, and also transmits information outward. Some of this information is received, stored, and transmitted as colour.

Our inner world is one of light and colour. What we identify as our "psychology" relates to our emotional condition and mental realm. Colour not only affects our physical state but also affects and reflects our emotional and mental states. We use colour within language to describe our state of being, for example: being in the pink, seeing red, green with envy, having the blues, black with despair, a yellow streak, and so forth.

Close your eyes. Can you see colours against a dark field? They can be geometric patterns or images. Colours represent different aspects of energy that relate particularly to our mental and emotional states. They can also be afterimages that result from exposure to bright light.

Some people are born with the ability to see astral colours, but you can also learn to see the colours of the astral aura. In either case, you still have to learn to interpret what you are seeing. When you know how to put the information together, you will recognize the colours and their symbolism, along with any feelings and emotions that you pick up from the person at whom you are looking. Soon you will be able to tell a great deal about people and their condition by the colours within their energy field. Even if you cannot pick up the knack of seeing the astral aura, you can get lots of clues about people's personalities by the colours they wear or have around them.

Our Energy Field

There are many layers within an aura, and each one has a slightly different structure and function, although they all store energy in different forms. The layer of the energy field that processes and stores information as colour is called the astral body. It is our body of light. This becomes a database of coloured images called thought forms that are linked with thoughts and sensory experience.

The thought forms that are held within the denser astral field are linked to our personality, body, and current life situations. These are the "vibrations" that other people sense and automatically tune in to during the course of daily life. On a more spiritual level, we hold thought forms at a higher vibrational frequency within our astral body. This process represents memories and experiences that we have brought into this world with us from previous lives or from those times that we spent in the spiritual realm between our previous lives.

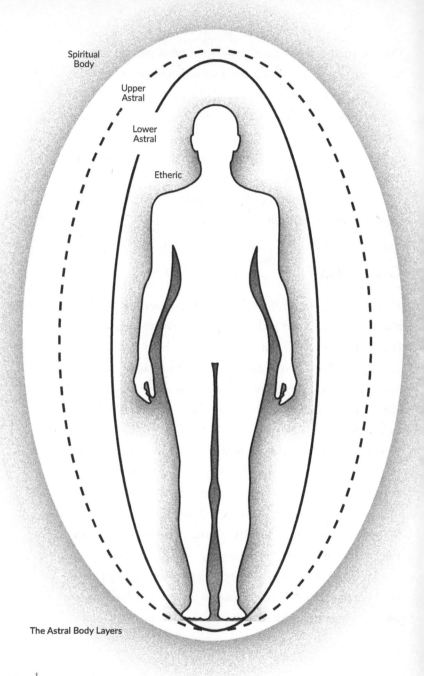

Spiritual Body

Upper Astral

Lower Astral

Etheric

The Astral Body Layers

These memories and experiences form a historical background of our life experiences and can be "drawn down" at times when they become relevant.

Everyone can sense the presence of others and even gauge their mood as part of the human survival strategy. Most people do not see the astral colours, though some people are born with this ability or develop it within their lifetime. Those who can see the astral body perceive it as a cloud of colours emanating from all life. In people, the astral body or field is egg-shaped. The colours move at different rates depending on how active that person is emotionally and mentally. Some colours remain the same throughout one's lifetime, and others change quite rapidly in reaction to the moment.

Colour and Karma

"Karma" is a Sanskrit word that means "action." It is the law of cause and effect or action and reaction that affirms that good or evil actions taken in one life determine one's condition in lives to follow.

The dominant colour of the denser astral aura is the energetic background that filters and influences the colours that appear in the rest of the aura. It represents our karmic pathway and personality characteristics, along with the nature of our life patterns and attitudes. This colour does not change through a person's life, and it shows the foundation of the soul lessons that dominate the personal life. The density and clarity of the colour show how positive the lessons are and where the person is in the course of his or her life journey. The colour tells about the assets a person brings into life as support while he or she is working through certain challenges.

Below are listed what I have found to be the personality characteristics and the past life patterns from which they emanate. The soul of the individual, prior to incarnation, chooses several incarnations with the same type of difficulties arising. This determines the life lessons and life circumstances of the individual, and the experiences are reflected in the dominant colour of the individual.

Most people who come for readings are interested in spiritual matters. Their auras show green, turquoise, blue, and some violet as their dominant colours. People with red and orange as their dominant colours are too busy making a success of it in the world to bother with readings, while people with yellow as their dominant colour have to see it to believe it—they are professional skeptics! See which one you relate to.

Dominant Red

The keyword is "sensation." The red type of person lives for the moment. These people are reflexive, responsive, and active. They are young souls who need to experience a great deal within the world. They can be ingenuous and innocent while also being crude and aggressive. They need a great deal of physical activity in their work and play, they are great sportsmen and women, and they have an interest in military matters. They can be very pioneering, as they have little fear of new things and they are willing to take physical risks. Committed to action, they are not deep thinkers. They can have volatile tempers, and they need to learn self-control. They can be selfish and irritable, but also very loving, as long as their needs are met.

Dominant Orange

The keyword for the orange type of person is "social ambition." These people come into life with the need to learn to work within a harmonious social context. In past lives, because of personal selfishness, they acted as disrupters of social progress. They have to learn to contribute to the group as a whole and to use their energies in positive ways to motivate others. They have a need to be active in community work and in politics. They achieve social status through hard work. People who have orange as their dominant colour have some problems being consistently strategic in how they go about things, and they can be sidetracked into doing too many things at the same time. They can also be very egotistical. They may appear to lose out when it comes to authenticity, trying to please all people and ending up pleasing none. On the plus side, they can be very motivating characters who manage to inspire people to get things done.

Dominant Yellow

The keyword of people whose dominant colour is yellow is "logical." In past lives the dominant yellow person was intensely emotional and had no respect for systems, the law, or rational thinking. These people threw tantrums, were dishonest, and might have reverted to substance abuse. In this lifetime, they are "professional skeptics" who question everything and have an "If I can't see it or touch it, it does not really exist" attitude. They need to be systematic and organized, and they are interested in proof. They think they are intellectual, though they can be pedantic and stubborn. Dominant yellow people approach everything as a problem to be solved. They like to argue. They make good attorneys, accountants, and statisticians. Very good at detail and precision work, they can be found working as dental technicians or watchmakers. They are not necessarily creative. They work better alone than within a team. They are strong willed and they tend to be judgmental about themselves and others. They need to be right. Dominant yellow people need to learn to commit to joy, humour, and playfulness, which are the positive aspects of the yellow ray.

Dominant Green

The keyword for people whose dominant colour is green is "trust." In past lives, dominant green people tended to be very selfish, inconsiderate, and self-centered. They assumed others would support them no matter how little they contributed to the community. In this life, dominant green people feel they have a mission in life beyond themselves.

They tend to be "other" oriented. They are here to learn to attain balance between what they give to others and what they allow themselves.

People with green as their dominant colour also have a problem with getting the balance right between independence and dependence in their life relationships. They have to learn to be properly nurturing and not overly motherly (this applies to men and women) and to allow others to make mistakes. Dominant green people make great teachers, therapists, craftspeople, and gardeners, and they can turn their hand to anything practical. Everyone comes to them with their problems because they have a lot of common sense and they can give good advice. They need to be in the middle of things, they are very active, they accomplish a great deal, and they are natural-born leaders. Above all, though, they need to learn to accept help from others. Greens are there for everyone else, and they feel bad because no one is there for them when they need them. This is because they don't let others help them, as they do not want to feel obligated! They also need to learn how to take leadership roles willingly and how to delegate.

People whose dominant colour is green need to be loved and needed and have a terrible time saying no. They need to learn to affirm their boundaries and acknowledge themselves and their accomplishments as well as their own needs. They need to learn about trust issues, such as whom to trust and whom not to trust, and above all—how to trust themselves.

Dominant Turquoise

The keyword for the dominant turquoise soul is "freedom." In past lives, dominant turquoise people tended to be very rigid in character and very involved with their nuclear families. In this life, they need to learn flexibility and tolerance, and they need to discover that there are many ways of approaching life. People whose dominant colour is turquoise are often the black sheep of their families, they don't feel like they fit in, and they have itchy feet. Intensely curious and impatient, they are quick learners. They often move away from their natural family and proceed to make their own family from friends. They love to travel, they have many friends from foreign countries, they have the gift of gab, and they are wonderful raconteurs.

People whose dominant colour is turquoise often marry out of their class, religious upbringing, or nationality. They take delight in being rebellious or slightly shocking. Their role is to be a catalyst in relationships—to make things happen and then to withdraw. They are jacks-of-all-trades, and as they can't stay still for long, they succeed only when setting and reaching short-term goals, or they become distracted and move on to the next exciting possibility. They are gregarious and are good at getting others to talk about themselves, yet they do not reveal much about themselves. They seem to be laid back, but they are quite good at hiding their true feelings. Always taking notes inside their heads, they are intensely perceptive about others. Their downside is a fear of commitment, a lack of tenacity, boredom, and escapism.

Professionally speaking, dominant turquoise types are good writers, journalists, and reporters. They are interested in words and languages and have an affinity with the travel industry, sales, marketing, public relations, networking, inventing, film, photography, sculpture, and dance. They need to learn to respect their role at the surface of life and to learn to be free even in the midst of commitments.

Dominant Blues: Sky Blue and Indigo

The keyword for these old souls is "truth." In past lives they have been in positions of power and responsibility but have misused their positions for personal gain. In those past lives, they were educated and privileged, and they were aware that they were going against the spiritual and secular law. They come into this life with a burden of guilt, and they worry about getting things right or wrong.

People whose dominant colour is blue dislike making decisions, preferring to know that the outcome is safe before taking the plunge. They hate anyone telling them what to do, and they hate telling themselves what to do. They need to learn to take control of themselves by learning to make decisions from their inner life rather than their wholly rational side. They drive themselves and everyone else crazy with their decision-making problem.

Dominant blue people do not like periods of transition. They are like an on-off switch, as they are either doing all or doing nothing. They cannot cope with shades of gray. They like to be the power behind the throne and to watch from the sidelines before committing themselves to actions or words. They will keep things bottled up until they explode, so they need to learn to communicate.

Blues are great at perceiving patterns. They are very creative, and they need to be doing something that involves mental design and patterns. Once they have done the mental work, however, they will ask someone else to do the dirty work. They tend to be quite psychic and sensitive and are fascinated by spiritual matters, but they often fear them. They are true-blue loyal. They find it hard to make friends and hard to let go of relationships or situations. They have stamina and staying power and are very focused. They prefer doing one thing at a time and being with one person or with small groups of people. They don't like noise or crowds.

Dominant blue people like to travel, but only first class. They seek status because they know about it from previous lives. They have good taste, and though they can live simply, they love beautiful things. They can be tight with their money and then blow it on the spur of the moment. Their motto should be "To thine own self be true." If they can listen to their higher self and then act on what they hear with faith, then all their decision making will take care of itself and it will come from the right place.

People whose dominant colour is light blue are more sociable, and need others more than do those whose colours are darker blues. They often need to learn to feel comfortable by themselves. They are interested in beauty, fashion, antiques, the law, computing, accounting, management positions, psychology, interior design, medicine, politics, strategies, and social status.

People whose dominant colour is indigo are more self-centered; they can be loners or have only one partner for life; and they need space, as they are very sensitive. They are very interested in music, science, research, the paranormal, psychology, medicine, religion, and mysticism. They are more rigid in their outlook than people whose dominant colour is a lighter blue, and they suffer from power issues and can have trouble due to their need to be right.

Dominant Violet

The keyword for people whose dominant colour is violet is "power." These are the true eccentrics of the world. They are interested in the occult and spiritual nature of life, and they tend to be very fanatical in their pursuits. In past lives, they lived as hermits and outcasts and now have to develop ways of fitting into society. There are strong self-sacrificial elements to their nature, and they tend to work for large causes. They feel the need to work for humanity, but they cannot cope well with people on an individual basis. They have big egos and need to be in charge—or they are withdrawn and have psychic or psychological disturbances that disrupt their ability to lead normal lives. In some cases, power translates simply into the power to move or exist or survive in the world. These people can also be revolutionaries who are misunderstood in their own time, as their vision goes beyond what currently exists.

Colour and the Chakras

10

The chakras (centers of consciousness) are located down the center of the body. They are energy vortices that transmute vibrations up and down the frequency bands. They shift colours fairly rapidly and represent how an individual is dealing with the challenges of living. The colours in the astral body near the chakras relate to the recent past or to the future, depending upon the nature of the chakra in question. There are often a variety of colours within the chakra or in the field next to it, and the patterns of the colours can be interpreted as qualities of energy. Their location within an aura will show how the individual is applying those energies to the different areas of life, including physical, emotional, mental, and spiritual health.

Each of these major centers is concerned with a certain area of life, which may relate to the physical, emotional, mental, or spiritual state. Each governs an aspect of the physical body in association with an endocrine gland, the etheric body via the nervous system in association with a nerve plexus, and the astral body via colour. Knowing how each chakra functions in depth gives an understanding of an individual's physical, psychological, and spiritual state. This is an essential part of both healing and psychic work. A little effort goes a long way when working with chakra energies!

For the purposes of symbolism, there is an association between the progression of rainbow colours and each chakra, but any colour can be normal when found within a chakra, as it describes the energies being expressed at that time in the person's life.

The Basic Associations for the Chakras

Chakra	Endocrine Gland	Nerve Plexus	Colour	Musical Note
Root	Adrenals	Coccygeal	Red	C
Sacral	Gonads	Posterior sacral	Orange	D
Solar plexus	Spleen, pancreas	Solar plexus	Yellow	E
Heart	Thymus	Cardiac	Green	F
Throat	Thyroid, parathyroids	Brachial	Turquoise	G
Third eye	Pituitary	Sympathetic nervous system	Indigo	A
Crown	Pineal	Parasympathetic nervous system	Violet	B

Following is some basic information about the nature of each of the chakras. If you are able to see the chakra colours either with your eyes open or closed, you can interpret the colour you see and know how that person is using the energy of the chakra within his or her life. No colour is good or bad in a chakra. Colours reflect only what *is*—and they change when the person changes the attitude that creates the colour! There is no concept of normality or perfection, so there is no need for a person to have the colour that is associated with the chakra appearing within it—for instance, red in the root chakra. We are complex individuals, and our emotions change frequently. What one aims to achieve is clarity of colour, along with a balanced shape and ordered flow within the coloured astral field.

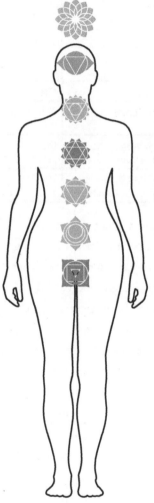

Crown Chakra: Violet

Third Eye Chakra: Indigo

Throat Chakra: Turquoise

Heart Chakra: Green

Solar Plexus Chakra: Yellow

Sacral Chakra: Orange

Root Chakra: Red

Root Chakra (*I*)

Location: The root chakra extends from just below the pubic bone to about halfway down the thighs. It has the slowest rate of rotation and is concerned with our survival in this lifetime.

Governs: The root center indicates the personal evolutionary cycle of the individual. Each cycle lasts about two and a half years and relates to a specific set of learning experiences that the individual must pass through. It also shows what the person attracts externally.

Psychic Function: Physical plane, survival.

Endocrine Gland: The adrenal glands are located above the kidneys in the midback. The adrenal glands govern fight-or-flight reactivity for survival in the physical world. This is the only chakra for which the endocrine gland is not directly over the chakra's physical zone.

Nerve Plexus: Posterior sacral plexus. The posterior sacral plexus governs the nerves of the large intestine, responsible for the elimination of solid waste. This relates to eliminating things that are no longer useful and to letting go.

Psychological: If you can see astral colours, then whatever colour or colours are present in the chakra will describe in detail the types of experiences that person is attracting to himself or herself. The chakra also tells about the basic health constitution of the individual. If the chakra is large, strong, and energetic, then the individual's constitution is strong, but if it is weak, then the person is constitutionally vulnerable. The energy state also tells how grounded and earthed that person is.

Colour: The colour red bears a metaphorical relationship to this center in that red represents pure energy. It is the lowest vibrational frequency of the spectrum, and it is hot, dense, and physical. It also represents the fight-or-flight reaction and nervous irritability. Too much red can be overstimulating.

Key Term: Physical survival.

The Colour Red in Any Chakra

Red in the root: dealing with anger while going through a cycle of sensation, getting off his or her backside and doing something, being more spontaneous

Red in the sacral: anger and frustration, issues with self and others

Red in the solar plexus: irritability and impatience with circumstances

Red in the heart: frustrated desires regarding the ability to change the person's life

Red in the throat: frustration with self-expression

Red in the third eye: drug irritations

Red in the crown: a situation in the future that will make the person angry

Sacral Chakra (*We*)

Location: The sacral chakra is located between the navel and the pubic bone.

Governs: The sacral chakra governs relationships.

Psychic Function: Physical plane or survival of the species through reproduction and relationships.

Endocrine Gland: The gonads—female ovaries and male testes. These glands ensure the perpetuation of the species. They also define our biological being and influence our sociological functions and activities, including the way we relate to our "self" and how others relate to us.

Nerve Plexus: Anterior sacral plexus. The anterior sacral plexus governs the generative organs as well as bladder function.

Psychological: How we manage ourselves in relationships is a key to personal growth and productivity in life. The center reflects how we relate to our gender identity. It also reflects our ability to be practically creative in our daily lives, as well as the manner in which we are able to cope emotionally with the world and appropriately let go of emotional problems.

Colour: Orange is the colour of ambition, politics and negotiation, and appetite and motivation.

Key Term: Relationships. The center governs and reflects first our relationship with our self and then the range of relationships we have with others.

The Colour Orange in Any Chakra

Orange in the root: period of time to work on ambition and motivation, work with groups

Orange in the sacral: learning diplomacy and negotiation skills in relationships

Orange in the solar plexus: active diplomacy and negotiation in the workplace

Orange in the heart: desire to work with and represent others in groups

Orange in the throat: speaking out in an advocacy role for others or for self

Orange in the third eye: spiritual ambition

Orange in the crown: developing new ambitions, working with groups

Solar Plexus Chakra (*I Will*)

Location: The solar plexus center is located in the soft tissue over the stomach, just below the breastbone.

Governs: The solar plexus center governs decision making.

Psychic Function: Emotional plane, clairsentience—the ability to have clear sensations in a psychic sense—for example, sensing ley lines and Earth energies—or duplicating physical sensations in one's body of what is happening in others.

Endocrine Gland: Pancreas and spleen. The pancreas governs the balance of available sugars in the blood. The spleen has an immune function and stores red blood cells. The connection between these glands and the solar plexus chakra relates to how energy is utilized by the body.

Nerve Plexus: Solar plexus. This nerve plexus governs the organs of digestion.

Psychological: Energy production and utilization are related to digestion of information. The way that we make choices depends upon the manner in which we take in information, break it down into component pieces, and then decide what to do with it—for example, store it, use it, or eliminate it.

Colour: Yellow is the colour that relates to mental processes, list making, and analysis.

Key Terms: Decision making, the choices made in living daily life.

The Colour Yellow in Any Chakra

Yellow in the root: period of time when there is the need to look at all life systems, paperwork, and finances, as well as a time of learning and study

Yellow in the sacral: developing understanding of personal needs through analysis and list making

Yellow in the solar plexus: joyful or analytical approach to things, learning new skills in workplace, studying

Yellow in the heart: desire to study, desire for more joy in life

Yellow in the throat: expression through facts and logic

Yellow in the third eye: restructuring the mind

Yellow in the crown: study, paperwork, or legal matters in the future

Heart Chakra (*I Feel*)

Location: The heart chakra is under the center of the breastbone in the middle of the chest.

Governs: The heart chakra governs the relationship to self, one's sense of life purpose, and empathy for others.

Psychic Function: Emotional plane, empathy, understanding others' feelings and motives.

Endocrine Gland: The thymus secretes and stores T-lymphocytes, which are responsible for a large portion of the body's immune response.

Nerve Plexus: Cardiac. The cardiac plexus governs heart and lung function. We cannot live without oxygen, and breathing and heart function go together to pump life force through the physical body, making life possible.

Psychological: Feeling good creates immunity; feeling bad creates vulnerability, not only emotionally but also physically. Circulation of the life force is more than a physical phenomenon. Air carries more than just life-force oxygen; it also carries the solar-electromagnetic charge to the body, which is circulated through the etheric body, making nerve function possible as well as storing vitality. The will to live with a sense of purpose and direction is a spiritual and psychological matter that is translated into physical activity. Feeling compassion for yourself and others aids the decision-making process.

Colour: Green is the colour of nature, nurture, and trust.

Key Terms: Connection with true self, balance.

The Colour Green in Any Chakra

Green in the root: a period of intense activity when trust in oneself is paramount, when you need to learn to delegate and be more balanced in meeting your own needs

Green in the sacral: friendship, the most important aspect of this time, to oneself and to others

Green in the solar plexus: practical application to material problems, security issues regarding decision making, developing confidence

Green in the heart: desire for family, desire to move or to decorate property

Green in the throat: speaking out on behalf of others, teaching

Green in the third eye: aspirations to new activities

Green in the crown: dealing with family or material matters or a move in the future

Throat Chakra (*I Express*)

Location: The throat chakra is located, simply, in the throat.

Governs: The throat chakra governs self-expression, speech, and conceptual creative activity.

Psychic Function: Mental plane, clairaudience—the ability to hear spirit voices clearly, as if they were standing close by and speaking in your ear.

Endocrine Glands: Thyroid and parathyroid glands. The thyroid gland is responsible for development of secondary sexual characteristics in maturity. It is also implicated in governing the rate of metabolic processes. The parathyroid glands regulate the amount of available calcium in the blood. Calcium is necessary for strong bones as well as nervous reactivity.

Nerve Plexus: Brachial. The brachial plexus governs the arms and the neck.

Psychological: Our neck allows us to broaden the scope of our vision, and our arms and hands allow us to manipulate our environment. The ability to reflect upon experiences, to make them one's own, and to have the courage to communicate them to others is necessary in order to mature and understand oneself. This process relates to our thyroid function. Metaphorically, parathyroid function relates to creating appropriate structures that lead to appropriate actions. Silent thought or spoken words structure activity.

Colour: Turquoise is the colour of freedom of expression and love of language.

Key Term: Self-expression.

The Colour Turquoise in Any Chakra

Turquoise in the root: a period of change, lightening up, expansion, exploration and risk taking, travel and foreign people in life

Turquoise in the sacral: need to expand social context, meet new people, and bring communication issues to the fore

Turquoise in the solar plexus: actively making changes and taking risks in work-related areas of life

Turquoise in the heart: desire to travel, to be more light-hearted

Turquoise in the throat: desire to be more communicative and creative

Turquoise in the third eye: seeking new experiences, vision of trying out new ways of being optimistic

Turquoise in the crown: period of change and playful expansion coming along

Third Eye Chakra (*I Have Vision*)

Location: Located in the brow between the eyes.

Governs: The third eye center governs inner vision, image making, and imagination.

Psychic Function: Mental plane, clairvoyance—the ability to see clearly, to see images, patterns, and colours. It also denotes understanding: "I see!"

Endocrine Gland: Pituitary. The pituitary is the master gland that secretes hormones to control the functions of the rest of the endocrine glands.

Nerve Plexus: Sympathetic nervous system. The sympathetic nervous system is responsible for stimulating involuntary life functions and primitive survival mechanisms—including the emotions.

Psychological: What we can see determines our viewpoints, beliefs, and actions, relating to the function of the pituitary gland. Our ability to see inner colour, to access memory via images, and to generate new images or image combinations allows us to have insights and creative drive to manage and manipulate our world.

Colour: Indigo is the colour of deep thinking, music, interest in the mysteries, and psychology.

Key Terms: Seeing and understanding.

The Colour Indigo in Any Chakra

Indigo in the root: a period of setting priorities and letting go of all that no longer has value, including relationships, situations, and things; interest in psychology

Indigo in the sacral: disillusionment in relationships, an inward time of learning to be alone

Indigo in the solar plexus: sitting back and seeing what happens, being receptive and deeply thoughtful and strategic before acting

Indigo in the heart: desire for quiet time and peace, desire to look into spiritual matters

Indigo in the throat: speaking up with strength at the right moment, singing ability

Indigo in the third eye: dreaming, psychic openness, time of vision and receptivity

Indigo in the crown: letting go of things and being more insular in the time to come

Crown Chakra (*Me and the Planet*)

Location: The crown center rises vertically from the center of the brain upward about five inches.

Governs: The crown center governs our sleeping and waking cycles, our relationship to available sunlight, and our relationship to Earth's magnetic north. The crown center shows patterns for potential manifestations in the future.

Psychic Function: Spiritual plane, intuition, or the ability to perceive the truth or facts without reasoning.

Endocrine Gland: The pineal gland is located in the center of the brain beneath the corpus callosum between the right and left brain.

Nerve Plexus: Sympathetic nervous system. The sympathetic nervous system is responsible for calming down involuntary life functions and primitive survival mechanisms—including the emotions.

Psychological: This is the only vertical chakra and therefore connects us to the planet and the stars. Our ability to navigate and be responsive to the subtleties of planetary existence is condensed within this center. The crown center also holds psychic information about what is to come into our life based on what has been seeded in our thought forms.

Colour: Violet is the colour of power over heaven and earth and otherworldly existence.

Key Terms: The future, relationship to the world.

The Colour Violet in Any Chakra

Violet in the root: going through a period of transformation and confronting old, deep-seated issues that may have been hidden; time to tap into personal power and spirituality; grieving or mourning

Violet in the sacral: transforming relationship with self and others by electing to be alone

Violet in the solar plexus: setting boundaries and being confrontational

Violet in the heart: desire to be involved with spiritual work or to withdraw for a period of time

Violet in the throat: either being very confrontational or very editing in self-expression

Violet in the third eye: being full of insight and inspiration, a time of powerful dreams

Violet in the crown: separation, a period of mourning, grieving, or Isolation in the future

Finally . . .

The proper functioning of these centers and the connections among them is vital to our ability to live and function effectively within the world. A trained therapist can help you to clear the chakras of blockages and gradually bring you to a higher state of functioning, using colour alone or in conjunction with other energy healing methods.

Develop Your Colour Awareness

11

This chapter will give you some concrete ways of exploring the meanings of the colours and developing your understanding through taking action and doing something practical rather than just reading about them! Some projects are more long term than others, but if you see them as experiments, through repetition you will develop your colour awareness in ways that can be applied in your own life as well as the lives of others.

The idea of making up a colour notebook may not appeal to everyone, but you may hope to work in fashion or decor or to produce art that is used in advertising or packaging.

If you wish to create a colour notebook, buy a ring binder so that you can add pages easily, and divide it into sections devoted to each colour. Cut out and add to your notebook magazine pictures featuring different colours. Take notes on things that you hear about different colours. Look at the complementary colours and related colours as a contrast. Make a chart of shades and tints taken from the bright colour, and make drawings using the range of tints and shades. Look for examples of clothing, makeup, fashion publicity, advertising materials, street signs, and decor, and make notes about them. Associate what you see with what you feel and think in relation to each colour.

One Colour Per Week

Concentrate your attention for one week on an individual colour. Every morning, stare at that colour for a few minutes and try to dress using that colour each day during the week. Buy flowers in that colour range, eat food of that colour, drink solarized water in that colour (see the chapter 15 "Healing with Colour"). Notice others who wear that colour, and make a note of their age group, attitudes, and outlooks. See whether (and how) your own feelings, sensations, and mood have been affected by wearing that colour. Add these impressions to your colour diary.

Practice some colour breathing (see chapter 15, "Healing with Colour"), eye-saturation exercises (staring at a colour until you almost draw it inside yourself), and meditations on that colour, and write down your experiences and observations. Draw pictures or doodle to reflect your feelings about that colour. Don't worry about what your artwork looks like; just play with the crayons, pencils, or paints and get into the mood! Let the colour express itself through you.

Draw pictures in that colour. You may even be able to choose music that expresses the colour and listen to it while relaxing and meditating or drawing. Composers use the chromatic scale to express musical ideas, and the word "chromatic" means "coloured." Some examples might be red for martial music, such as that played by military bands, or patriotic music, and blue for "the blues," quiet jazz, classical music by Debussy and Ravel, or romantic music. Yellow could represent Bach or electronic music, while green might relate to sentimental music or country music.

At the end of the week, reflect upon your experiences and create a summary of them.

Complementary Colour After-Image

Paste a coloured piece of paper on a white background. Stare at it for a while, then look to the side of it. You will see a pale colour floating next to it. This is the astral complementary colour. Now try looking at the coloured paper; then close your eyes and see what colour the afterimage becomes. Green may follow red, or yellow may follow another colour. The purpose of this exercise is to help you to see astral colour and to give you an experience of the complementary colours.

Feeling Colours

Buy a book of multicoloured craft paper. Lay the sheets of various colours out on a table. Close your eyes and move your hands slowly above the sheets of paper. Observe any feelings or sensations you have in relation to the different colours. Doing this without looking will help you to focus on your nonvisual experiences.

With your eyes closed, hold each colour in front of each of your chakras and observe any changes in sensation or feeling you have in association with individual colours. You may surprise yourself!

There is a fascinating story about an airline that found itself experiencing an unusually high incidence of passengers getting airsick. Airline representatives consulted doctors and psychologists and eventually came to the conclusion that the orange and tan colour scheme inside the cabins of their aircraft was causing the problem. They changed the colour scheme to various shades of blue, and the number of airsick passengers dropped dramatically!

Candle Meditation Exercise

Candle flames symbolize the light of spirit reaching upward. Although the flame is always the same colour, using coloured candlesticks symbolically influences the light that is burning. By meditating on the candle, you begin to develop your third eye chakra and sensitize your inner vision. This will also help you develop clairvoyance as well as develop the ability to see auras.

Buy candlesticks in each colour of the spectrum. Place a candle in a position where it burns at eye level, on a table opposite you in a darkened room. Sit comfortably in an upright position. With your eyes closed, begin to breathe slowly, deeply, and rhythmically. When you feel relaxed and centered, open your eyes, and look *past* the candle flame so that it lies in the center of your field of vision. Do not gaze at it directly; let your gaze look through the candle. Keep relaxing and gazing, breathing in the light and associating it with the colour of the candlestick. Breathe in the coloured light toward your eyes and nose as if you were drawing it into your body. Hold your breath comfortably and exhale slowly through closed teeth, making a hissing sound. Then repeat the cycle.

When you tire of making the hissing sound, or if the pressure around your third eye (in the forehead area) becomes too great, exhale through your nose. When your eyes become tired, close them and try to keep the bright afterimage centered in your field of vision until it fades completely.

Repeat the candle gazing twice more. When you finish, rub the palms of your hands together vigorously and cup them over your open eyes, feeling the exchange of heat and energy into the muscles.

Seeing Auras

I was born with the ability to see the aura or energy field, and I truly cannot turn it off. Most people cannot see the colours within the energy field, but it is a skill that can be learned with practice and patience. Most people can see the etheric field, which is the colourless glow that runs from around three to five inches from the body. When people are full of vitality, it glows brightly, but when they are depleted, it is smaller and misty gray.

The astral field stores energy as colour, and what you will be attempting to see is that layer. It extends to about three to five feet around the body in an egg shape. The colours are not bright but cloudlike and subtle, more like the colours you see when doing the complementary colour eye-saturation exercise. This makes it advisable to do that exercise and the candle meditations before attempting to look at the aura, as the exercises will give you some idea of what you should be looking for.

Seeing auras is basically a matter of how you focus your eyes. When looking at an object or a person, the tendency is to use convergent vision so that both eyes are focusing on a point. Each eye has a slightly different field of vision, and when these fields come together they overlap in the center and also add a little extra distance at the periphery. To see the aura, you need to use divergent vision—as if the eyes are looking slightly outward and in different directions. You do this naturally when you focus on something behind an object. The object becomes included in the whole of the larger picture even though you are not looking directly at it. It also occurs when you are "spacing out" and letting your gaze be unfocused.

You can practice by looking at a person sitting opposite you. Look beyond the person with a relaxed gaze, around eight to ten inches around his or her body and particularly above and around the head and over the chakras. You may see a flash of colour or you may start out by seeing misty, moving energies that suggest colour.

Keep your eyes relaxed. At first you will be shocked by the flash of colour and try to focus on it. That will not work! You may already have experienced this with the complementary colour exercise by finding that your eyes jump around too much or that when you tried to focus, the colour slipped away. Try not to become frustrated or to give up. After all, you have been focusing on the world with convergent vision since you were an infant, so you will need some practice to extend the way in which you use your eye muscles. Once you have begun to see the colours, it will become easier to see more detail and you will be able to become more relaxed. The next step is interpreting what you see, and you can refer to the relevant chapters in this book to help you with that process.

Art Project

Buy a set of tubes of gouache or watercolour paints, brushes, and a mixing tray. On a sheet of white paper, make a square of a bright colour. To the right of the bright colour, progressively dilute the colour with water, making brushstrokes and then diluting again until there is hardly any colour left. The progressively paler colours are called tints.

On the same side, repeat this process, but instead of diluting the saturated colour with water, dilute its intensity by adding white progressively, until the colour returns to white. Repeat this process to the left of the bright colour, but progressively add black to the bright colour. The addition of white or black creates shades.

Give your tints and shades names. This will help you to become sensitive to the differences in the secondary colours—for example, red-orange or orange-red, and the way that they change when mixed with white and black. See how you relate to the physical and psychological impact of these colours.

Playing with Colour Mixtures

Colour pervades your world. Certain colours attract or repel you. Colour affects what you buy and how you perceive and judge others. Advertising and marketing companies have done a huge amount of research on the psychology of colour. For example, a book that has not sold well under a cover of a particular colour might do better with a cover of a different colour. In the same way, manufacturers sometimes change the colour on their "new and improved" products. We get the message visually first and then through the advertisers' words. Every shade of colour sends us a message and describes states of being. When seeking to understand something in depth, we look for "shades of meaning."

When looking at mixed colours and shades, we break the shade down into its primary colours and note whether white or black has been added.

For Example: Apricot

Contains: Orange = Yellow + Red

Tint: Apricot = Yellow + Red + White

Shade: Burnt orange = Yellow + Red + Black

It is important to note that orange can be either red-orange or yellow-orange, meaning that the first colour of the mixture creates the secondary colour and dominates the outcome.

Guidelines for Understanding Mixtures

Colours are neither good nor bad. They denote energy states that are active and outgoing or receptive and inward turning. We are all able to judge whether the colour that is used is appropriate for its purpose or not.

- Bright, saturated colours—both primary and secondary—are outgoing and active, for example, fire-engine red or sunflower yellow.

- When we interpret the meaning of a colour, the dominant colour of the secondary combination becomes more influential, for example, red-orange.

- Whenever white or black is added to a colour, it progressively dilutes that colour until it is completely absorbed by the white or the black.

- Whenever a saturated colour has white added to it, the psychological impact becomes more innocent, ethereal, or insipid.

- When a saturated colour has black added to it, the psychological impact becomes more earthy, heavy, and repressed.

Dress for Success

12

In our fashion-conscious world, not only style but also colour communicates volumes of information about us to others.

We tend to spend some time selecting our clothes, purchasing them, and choosing what to wear for particular occasions. We wear different garments for doing daily chores than we do when we go out on a trip, go to work, or attend a fancy occasion. We all have our particular comfort zone with regard to colours that we choose to wear—or not to wear.

Your Personal Colour Experiment

Keep a pen and paper beside you when doing this visualization exercise.

Sit comfortably and picture your clothes closet. In your mind's eye, go through the clothing hanging there. What are the dominant colours? What colours are missing? Now, in your mind's eye, look into every drawer in your chest of drawers and see what colours predominate and also see whether, again, there are any colours missing.

Now, imagine laying out all your clothes into three piles:

- Leisure clothes

- Business clothes

- Play clothes, both semiformal and formal

In your mind's eye as you look through your wardrobe, do you see any patterns regarding the colours?

Is there a difference between the colours in your summer and those in your winter wardrobe?

Now, remembering this information, open your eyes and jot down your impressions.

What do you notice about the range of colour in your wardrobe? Look up the meanings of those colours and figure out the messages you are sending out in these areas of your life. Write all these insights down next to your notes. Consider whether the signals you are sending out are ones that you intend to send out or that you want to send out. Believe it or not, you can choose the messages you transmit by consciously choosing the colours you wear.

Power Dressing

There is often a different range of colours for each of your activities. This is already reflected in your wardrobe.

- Party clothes are probably brighter because you are going out with the intention of having a good time.

- Formal wear is often black with bright accents.

- For a sophisticated image, plain colours of any shade are better than prints.

Some simple guidelines in choosing colour tones to keep in mind are:

- If you want to be seen as serious, wear darker colours.

- If you want to project a younger and more frivolous message, wear pastel tints.

- If you want to appear more assertive and upbeat, wear saturated bold colours.

Hot Stuff, Baby

Hot colours are reds, yellows, and oranges. All these colours are stimulating, dynamic, and extroverted. They encourage interaction and external activity. This is true whether the colour is saturated, a shade, or a tint. Red and shocking pink are considered to be sexy colours.

Cool Dudes

Cool colours are blues and violets. These colours are receptive and introverted. They encourage introspection, a more reserved sense of personal space, and self-control. They are wonderful colours to dress a small child in as they promote calmness.

Even Steven

Green is the colour of balance in that it combines warm yellow and cool blue. The proportion of yellow to blue will determine whether the green is more stimulating or more calming. Green can be considered to be a colour that promotes balance.

Colours and Patterns

Fabric can be plain or patterned. Patterns can be geometric, freeform, or floral. Patterns add interest to fabric and provide the opportunity to use more colours. Fabric patterns can be generated from a weave, such as jacquard, herringbone, or plaid, or from printing on plain fabric. Some fabrics combine geometric and floral patterns, and these are often found in "ethnic style" clothing. Bright, bold colours in patterns are busy and extroverted, sending out a message that says, "Look at me!" Geometric patterns give a more directed or structured image, and floral patterns are more feminine, even if the colours are bold and bright rather than subtle. Small patterns send out a message of attention to detail and subtlety, while large, bold patterns send the message of assertion and a flamboyant approach.

Look carefully at the combinations of colours and patterns in your own clothing to determine what message you are sending out.

Accent Colours

By using bright or pastel colours, you can personalize even the most conservative look and convey a message. For example, at a job interview, you need to consider the kind of message you wish to give. If you wear a navy suit that projects a conservative image, you might augment that message by choosing the following shirt:

Pastel flowers: Feminine

Plain pastel colour: Conservative

Bold, plain colour: Assertive

White shirt or striped shirt: Powerful and masculine

Bold geometric print in varied colours: Individualistic

If you wear a tie or scarf, the same categories apply. By wearing a navy suit and pastel shirt, you are conveying a conservative and low-key image, but by adding a tie or a scarf that has a bold geometric print in blue shades and blue tints, you are also saying that you are logical and that you have good, individual style.

So, always consider the occasion and the message that you wish to convey.

Uniforms Mean Business

Uniforms exist so that people are seen not as individuals but as part of a group. The uniform presents a corporate image. The following colours are frequently found in uniforms, and they can be consciously or unconsciously applied. They can be formal outfits, such as suits, or even casual ones, such as those that include denim.

Choose the image you wish to project consciously from the following list for business interviews or meetings where you wish to project a particular persona.

- **Navy** is the colour most often worn by financiers, police officers, and lawyers. Blue symbolizes the higher conceptual pattern of the universe, and the dark shade adds weight to that expression. Navy conveys the message "You can trust me because I can see what's going on here and I can deal with it."

- **Black** is the colour most often worn by the clergy and by classical musicians. It conveys a message of connection to the great mystery of life. The person himself or herself is hidden. Black also covers up the lumps and bumps of life, and as it is all-absorbing, it offers a message of special knowledge and of hidden power. Think of the little black dress!

- **White** is the colour most often worn by the medical profession, laboratory scientists, and catering staff. It is the colour of purity and conveys a message of cleanliness and pristine order. It gives off a cool, godlike, untouchable message.

- **Gray** is a colour favored by bureaucrats and managers, as it is neutral and it operates as a smoke screen to hide behind so no one can "see your hand." It does not convey the drama of black or white, so it is effective for negotiations, especially for situations in which you do not wish to appear threatening.

- **Brown** is the colour of security. It is down-to-earth, slightly hidden, but symbolic of someone who is practical and who gets things done.

- **Patterned** suits are often worn by salespeople because the active pattern keeps the energy moving between them and their clients. This also applies to men's sports jackets in tweed or plaid, such as those worn by teachers. They are seen as slightly more informal, and they encourage dialogue.

You and Your Colours

Now you can consciously select colours for specific purposes. You can wear red socks in winter to warm your feet! You can promote a bright, positive, feel-good factor by including warm colours in your clothing. You would come across as a cooperative team player if you elected to wear greens and brown. You can exert a sense of cool, confident control in blues. You can also use clothing to help develop sides of your nature that are unexpressed.

Likes and Dislikes and What They Mean

If you find that you have nothing of one particular colour in your wardrobe, and if you believe that you do not like that colour, you are demonstrating that you have a problem with the energy qualities that the colour represents. By consciously including in your wardrobe some items of that colour, beginning with accents in prints or accessories, you will begin to get in touch with the energy of the colour. This is a very therapeutic thing to do.

You may find that you have items of that colour in your environment, but they may not exist within your wardrobe. Clothes represent a direct reflection of our connection to ourselves. On the other hand, our environment, though it relates to our personal expression, is one step removed from our personal sense of self.

Choose Colours that Look Good On You

All skin tones are within either the yellow or the blue range. People with yellow-based complexions look better in blue tones, and people with blue-based complexions look better in yellow-tone. Think about compliments you get on a colour you are wearing. Consider how much of that colour you have in your wardrobe and whether there should be more of it! Some colours drain the colour from your face. A lot depends on your skin colour, but your hair and eye colour also have an influence.

- Dark hair, dark eyes, and dark skin can wear bright, saturated colours and pastel colours.

- Dark hair, light eyes, and pale skin can wear bright colours.

- Fair hair, dark eyes, and dark skin can wear shades.

- Fair hair, light eyes, and pale skin can wear pastel colours.

Think about how you *feel* in the colours you are wearing. If you are unhappy with particular colours, you can change in order to *feel* better. In other words, there will be more harmony between your sense of who you are at that moment in time and how you wish to interact with the world.

If you want others to see the real you, choose colours that send out the right message!

People Are the Colours They Choose

We are all people watchers—whether we admit it or not. This is a natural part of our survival strategy and is often an unconscious impulse. In fact, a great deal of the information that we perceive about others is subconsciously collected and bypasses what might be called our normal mental faculties. This is because we cannot process all that information at once! The information that we receive is a mixture of body language, tone of voice, smell, and physical contact, such as handshakes or casual touches. We also notice eye contact and movements—in addition to eye colour. We notice colour in a person's physical makeup as well as in what he or she is wearing or how he or she has decorated a personal space.

Colour relates to personal expression. It tells a story about a person's self-esteem and confidence, as well as the image that person is trying to project. After all, we all take care when buying clothes or when choosing what to wear on a daily basis. If you know a person well, then you can probably make an assessment of the range of colours that person usually wears. You can tell a lot about an individual's personality based on his or her colour choices. You may find that there are different colour ranges based on the types of activities the person is involved in. For instance, holiday and leisure wear tends to be bright; formal dressing can be darker and bolder; work attire can be more muted depending on the type of work or on whether the individual has a choice regarding work clothing. If the person works in a dangerous situation where it is important that he or she can be seen, a reflective red, orange, or yellow jacket is often required.

When looking at your friends, loved ones, and coworkers, note changes in the colours they wear, and see what they are telling you about changes in their lives. How conscious are they of the changes in colours they wear?

By knowing your colours, you can assess a person's mood, motives, and consciousness.

Ask Yourself the Following Questions:

1. What colours would you wear to make the best impression in the following situations?

   - A job interview for an advertising company

   - A job interview as an executive

   - A hot date

   - An afternoon outing in the city

2. What colours would you choose to:

   - Look sexy?

   - Look nonthreatening?

   - Look powerful and assertive?

   - Look thinner?

   - Create an impact?

   - Disappear?

3. If you want to emphasize a part of your body by wearing a colour, what tone of colour and range would you choose?

4. If you want to hide a specific area of your body by wearing a particular tone or colour, what would you choose?

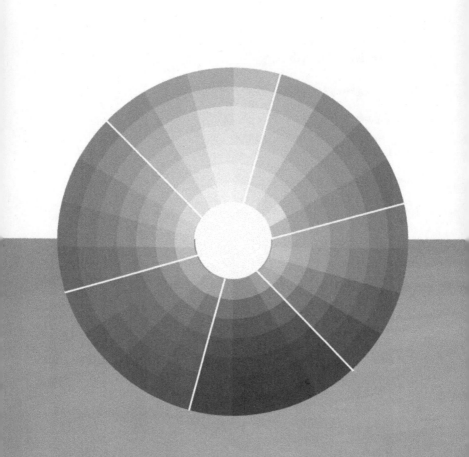

Décor

13

We live in privileged times and we take colour in our environment for granted. In ancient times, colour represented power. The original colours used for clothing and decor were derived from coloured mineral deposits or from vegetable sources. Those who had power and status could afford clothing, jewellery, and palaces that were adorned with colour and wrought metals, such as gold, silver, copper, and bronze.

This privilege extended to decorations in public function rooms where use of colour pointed to the particular function and where it made strong impressions. Dark colours with bold accents on walls, floors, and furnishings along with plenty of metal and artificial light created the drama necessary to impress and to make a statement about the wealth and power of the ruler.

The common people wore colours that they could dye with the vegetables they had at hand, and the poorer they were the less colour appeared in their clothes. Different eras had their preferred colour-ways, and their colours symbolized the growth and decline of economies:

- In the Middle Ages, red stood for courage and purity.

- In the seventeenth century, the vogue was for pastel colours.

- In the eighteenth century, the advent of trade brought the beginning of foreign-influenced decorative objects that were further developed in the nineteenth century.

- The nineteenth century and the blossoming of the Industrial Revolution brought décor into the homes of the growing middle classes.

Later in the nineteenth century, there was an explosion of changing styles. This came partly from the various influences that were around at that time and partly from the advances that had been made in the creation of inorganic dyes. This brought into being the lilacs of art nouveau, the earth tones of the English arts and crafts movement, the exotic iridescent colours of the Orient, and the sleek, industrial look of the modernist movement with its monochrome palette. The advent of electric lighting and artificial dyes changed what people saw and how people related to their environments. The new aniline synthetic dyes influenced the fashions of soft furnishings and decor as well as clothing. Colourwise, virtually everything became possible and available to ordinary people.

During the twentieth century, wealth became more evenly distributed, products became more available, people's lives became more mobile, and public awareness became more influenced by advertising. The beginning of the century was a time of pastel and floral colours. The 1920s were noted for the introduction of beige, along with pale, lustrous materials, sleek, shiny surfaces ornamented with metals, and glowing indirect light. Wartime colours were more subdued, with bright accents. Postwar colours were pink and bold, bright, glowing jewel tones. The '60s and '70s brought bold colour schemes along with all kinds of experimentation with synthetic materials. We are now in a time of mixing old and new and of experimenting with colour on a grand scale. Now we are all kings and queens as far as colour choice is concerned. With all the choice that is available, how strange that the supposedly stylish homes that are photographed for the weekend newspaper supplements are invariably white on white on white. They're boring, but probably easier to photograph than colour might be.

Vital Assessments

When you decorate a space, some vital points need to be assessed that will help you choose your colours. Consider the space itself: its shape, its function, and its exposure to natural light. Colour has a psychological impact, so choosing colours with these things in mind will help reduce stress in an environment, prevent accidents, or enliven a space. Is there a period theme to which you wish to adhere, based perhaps on the age of the property or your own preference? These are the things you need to take into consideration.

Light and darkness are the ultimate decorating statement; they make or break the colour or patterns of a room. They create drama and are ultimately of tremendous importance from a practical standpoint. Whether one uses white light or coloured bulbs, direct overhead lighting, up-lighting or lamps, the ambiance of a space is always affected by the lighting.

Assess how much the room is exposed to natural sunlight during the day. If the room faces east or west, it may receive sunlight only in the morning or afternoon. Light radically changes the appearance of colours. The shape of a room also has some bearing, as light may be angled more strongly in some areas depending upon the position of the windows, doors, and alcoves. This needs to be taken into consideration based on the function of the room, because by manipulating colours cleverly, you can make a space seem larger or smaller.

- Colours also look different in artificial light.

- Fluorescent north light has a blue bias. Most fluorescent

lighting in stores, factories, and offices is "daylight," which has a yellow-orange bias. It is bright and encourages efficiency.

- Households use warm white fluorescent tubes. This light's spectrum is biased toward orange to pink wavelengths and gives poor colour rendering.

- Tungsten lightbulbs have a strong red bias.

- Candles give off a yellow-pink or peach light that is very flattering.

The Colour Basics

- Warm colours advance and close a space in.

- Cool colours recede and increase the feeling of space.

- The more intense a colour is, the more we notice it.

- Using too many colours unbalances the effect.

- Metallic or glossy surfaces attract the eye and make colours brighter.

- Choose a colour theme that binds all the elements in the space together.

- If you are not confident when choosing decor, keep to no more than four colours in a room, including white for paint-work or vinyl window frames.

Refer to Your Colour Wheel

- Opposites or complementary colours enhance each other and make each appear more intense so they seem to glow against each other.

- Colours that are near each other on the colour wheel are harmonious, as they have elements in common, so they work well together. For instance, purple-blue-red is one combination, as is plum-red-orange-blue.

- Using different colours of the same tone or intensity gives a dramatic contrasting effect. For instance, pumpkin orange works with red, blue, and green, and midtone green works with forest green, dark red, and navy.

The amount of colour used and where it is placed can create a dramatic or subtle effect. Used in large areas, the colour creates the overall atmosphere; in small areas it acts as an emphasis or focal point. If you want to make a room look smaller, use warm colours. To open up or enlarge a room, use cool colours. If you have a high ceiling you wish to make seem lower, paint the walls a dark colour to picture-rail height, with white above and continuing over the ceiling. If you want to lower the ceiling, paint it a dark colour. Colour also gives a sensation of movement and perspective by leading the eye.

Mood Combinations

The mood combinations you choose have a great deal to do with the function of the room as well as the atmosphere that you want

to create, which may be formal or informal, personal or imper-
sonal, warm and cozy or cool and spacious.

- Dark tones tend to advance and make a room feel smaller and more personal.

- Wood tones, dark reds, purples, and browns are luxurious and tend to feel more masculine.

- Dark tones can be warm or cool in their elements.

- Pastel colours tint in light, and soft tones recede, giving fresh, airy feel and softness to a room. They are under-stated, tend to be more relaxing, and seem more restful.

Patterns and textures can be used to change the feel of a space in the following ways:

- Large, bold-coloured motifs attract the eye, so use them in areas you wish to bring forward.

- Small, muted patterns tend to merge into an over-all texture.

- Verticals give an impression of height, while horizontals widen a space.

- Textures emphasize the general effect given by a colour.

- Textures can also break up and disguise physical surface imperfections.

- Hard, glossy finishes are associated with streamlined effi-ciency so tend to look cold, especially with cool colours.

- Traditional surfaces such as soft, grainy wood and rich-textured fabrics suggest age and enhance the effect of reds, oranges, and browns.

You can use a single colour scheme by employing one colour in many shades and tones as well as in textures and patterns. Within a limited palette of monochromes, use the colours and textures of nature to create interest. Browns are based on earth pigments and have many variations of tone that go together. For example, wood, bamboo, matting, woven sisal, and so on all have different tones and textures of beige and brown. Mix shiny effects with matte ones.

A monochrome range is more sophisticated. Using complementary colours in the same tonal range makes for a dynamic contrast. Highlight with bright or dark tones as focal points within the room. Neutral tones can be brightened with colour accents. You can change the effect of a paint or wall colour by manipulating the following:

- Try a textured wallpaper or fabric, or paint over a patterned surface.

- Use a powdery matte effect or try a gloss or sheen.

- Historic colours and finishes use different carriers, such as milk, chalk, lime wash, rag rolling, sponging, marbling, trompe l'oeil, and distressed surfaces.

- Futuristic colour treatments might include unusual paints, metallic finishes, or pearl effects.

Metals are important accents in furniture and lighting fixtures, so consider the following:

- Gold is the colour of the sun and is warm and masculine. Use with dominant warm colours or to warm up a cool space.

- Silver represents the moon and is feminine and cool. It gives a more distant feeling to a space and can cool down a warm space. This applies also to office furniture or modern furniture that is made of steel or chrome.

- Copper, verdigris (copper with a patina), and bronze all are warm metals that are feminine in nature.

Colours change with distance. Objects moving away lose their colour before they lose their shape. Red, yellow, and orange are good safety colours because of their excellent visibility at a distance.

Colours are also associated with a place and reflect the climate and light. For instance, Mediterranean colours are clean and bright, while we associate Africa with reds and browns, and the Caribbean with bright primary and neon colours. You can evoke a place or an era by choosing a colour scheme that suggests that place or time.

Warm Colours

Red is a very versatile colour, which at full strength is dramatic and powerful. Yellow is the colour of sunshine and summer, so it adds visual warmth. Oranges cheer the heart. Use yellow and orange to give life to rooms that receive little natural light.

Clear pastel tints create a gentle ambiance for bedrooms or bathrooms. Use bright hues for a bolder effect. A light yellow tends to give a fresh look that can appear surprisingly cool, while red-orange can look even more dramatic when teamed with complementary blue colours. These shades also look good with wood or with metals such as copper, gold, and pewter.

Use red sparingly as an accent colour to warm a room; don't use too much or your room will look like a brothel—unless you are actually designing a brothel, that is! Dark reds are very masculine, sexy, and assertive, and they appear physically comfortable because they are warm yet stimulating. Red creates a sense of denseness and concentration, yet it is very active. It wants to get down to business—of one sort or another. Use red to attract attention to an area.

Orange is a good colour to use in public areas, as its warmth promotes good social interaction and feelings of comfort. It is good also for dining rooms and kitchens, and it helps "structure the fire" of an environment. Pale peach or apricot can be used in a playroom or nursery as a nurturing colour because it promotes good relationships and is uplifting. Shades of orange warm up and give an earthy feeling to a room. Bright orange accents add zing to a room without being too irritating. Very large rooms can look terrific with a deep orange colour. Orange warms the space, makes it appear smaller, and creates liveliness in corridors or rooms that can lack intimacy. Try using orange with a tone of blue, which is the colour opposite orange, to achieve a softening and balancing effect.

Yellow has a stimulating effect on the mind. As a room colour, the more saturated tones can be uplifting and warming, bringing a sense of sunshine and joy into a room. Yellow is good in kitchens or public rooms, as it can stimulate discussion and help digestion, and a yellow study promotes intellectual activity. It is a good brightening accent colour. However, it is not good to use as a main wall colour in rooms that are used for relaxation such as bedrooms or bathrooms due to its stimulating effect on the mind.

Brown is earthy, relaxing, and warm—think of wood. Although there are many shades of brown, and indeed many hues based on the dominant primary colour in the brown, if the whole room is brown, then it will be textures rather than colour that will be seen as important. Brown is conservative and represents security. Using brown in the decor of a shop or bank sends a message that your business is safe and that the establishment can be relied upon. Brown shades are wonderful in natural wood and natural materials and anywhere where a warm, earthy, natural appearance is required. Feng shui suggests that wood is a great choice for a kitchen, as it counteracts both the fire (which feng shui represents by red) and the water (which is represented by black or blue) and thus creates balance.

Cool Colours

Blues and greens are relaxing to live with because they make up so much of our natural world. The sky is composed of a huge variety of constantly changing blues, as is the sea. A vast number of shades of green occur in plant life. They bring the breath of the outdoors into the room. Pale blues and greens give a cool, airy feel, and the deep bright tones give a more exotic effect. Remember that green is made up of blue and yellow, the cool and warm ends of the spectrum, and is therefore balancing. The combination of white and yellow-green is springlike. Feng shui suggests that some green is great in a child's room as it promotes health and growth.

Green is restful and relaxing to the nervous system. With a dominance of blue in the mixture, it is a good colour for bedrooms and living rooms. With a dominance of yellow, it is good as an accent colour, bringing springlike life energy into the space. Of course, one can always use plants, foliage, and flowers to bring the green energy into a place. Some say that the yard or garden should also be considered as a room within a property.

Variations of **sky blue and indigo** are sedating, cool, and relaxing. Turquoise is livelier, as it stimulates discussion and movement. Blues give a feeling of space. They are good for bedrooms or any other room in which you wish to relax. Too much blue can be dull, so use warm accent colours or white to maintain some dynamic contrast. Different shades of blue also work well together to add variety.

Purples are very strong colours for use when decorating a whole room. Purple has a powerful effect on the nervous system that can either be sedating or irritating, depending on how much red there is in the mixture. Purple is a good accent colour. It can be quite masculine and it can give a feeling of opulence and power to a room, whether a sitting room or bedroom. It is also a colour that is good for spiritual work such as meditation.

In decor, **black and white**, either alone or together, make a bold and dramatic statement. This combination can be seen as very masculine. All black is very womblike and gothic; all white is sterile and pure. Either colour can be relaxing but also unrelenting. Black and white together suggest a rhythm that dances before the eyes, because the patterns these colours create become more important than the colours themselves.

• • •

Here is an interesting story about colour. A friend of mine spent her pregnancy happily decorating her coming baby's bedroom in bright, cheerful primary colours with pictures of teddy bears and similar images. The baby was a poor sleeper, so she decided to try changing the colour of his room. She redecorated the space in very pale shades of lavender with white, and the baby slept well thereafter!

However, my own suggestion for a sleep-challenged child is to decorate his or her bedroom in blues, greens, and whites. This will help create a calm and balanced atmosphere. If even this doesn't work, wait until the child becomes a teenager and you will be sure that he or she will sleep through the night until lunchtime the next day!

By manipulating colour knowledgably, you can change your environment in such a way that your life and the lives of others are enhanced.

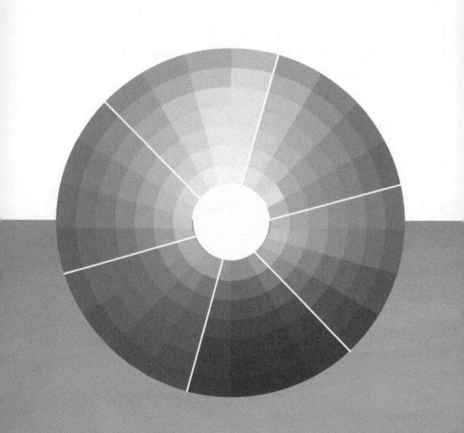

Colour
Divination

14

D ivination is the perception of the past, present, and future. It is fundamentally the ability to read patterns, make sense of them, and put the information together to create a coherent story. Some people (though none who are in the business) call it fortune-telling. There are many ways that colour is used in divination because colour is inseparable from all aspects of life. I mention here a few types of divination that specifically use colour—and provide brief descriptions.

Clairvoyance

Clairvoyance is the innate ability to perceive inner images. We all have this ability, but we call it our imagination. Learning to tap into this ability in a consistent and managed way is called clairvoyance. It is not an active imagination process through which we make up things in our mind that are then portrayed as images, but a process in which we create a blank screen upon which images from the subconscious mind are projected either randomly or in response to inner questions. Image structures can also be used to pin information on what we normally filter out of our field of consciousness.

Ribbon Reading

The technique of ribbon reading was developed extensively in pre-Victorian times. It was fashionable at the time for women to wear ribbons a great deal more than they do now, and ribbons were a very portable means of using colour references. If you want to do this for yourself, buy some ribbons of every colour of the rainbow, each being about twelve inches long, then tie a knot at one end of each ribbon. Have your subject ask a question, then tell the individual to close his or her eyes and concentrate on that question. Then, still with the eyes closed, tell the individual to choose one or more ribbons and then to hold them up by the knotted ends. You can then go on to interpret the colour and its meaning according to the question that the person asked.

Flower Reading

The charming method of flower reading was developed extensively in Victorian times as a throwback to previous eras when an appreciation of nature and colours was common. In this technique, a bouquet of flowers including every colour was created, along with the stems and leaves, and put into a vase. The querent needed to ask a question and then close his or her eyes. The bouquet was then placed in front of the individual, who was asked to draw out a flower. The flower that the person drew would be used in answer to the question. The "reader" interpreted the colour and form of the flower, its state of bloom, the number of leaves, and its lushness and freshness in relation to the question.

Card Systems

Many types of cards are used in divination. By shuffling the deck as you ask a question, you sort the cards by your own electromagnetic vibrations. The cards are cut or separated into three piles and re-formed into one deck, then laid out in a predetermined spread, where each area of placement has a particular meaning in time.

Divination is then possible by interpreting the meaning of the card in the place it lands in the spread in relation to the question asked.

Traditional card systems include playing cards with the four suits, each having a colour, image shape, and number associated with it that have specific combinations of meaning. The tarot uses more complex colours and image associations. There are many other types of modern cards, such as the goddess cards, angel cards, mermaid cards, and so on. The symbolic imagery and words used in each deck are different, but the way that each is used is exactly the same.

Colours on these cards relate to specific energy states, particularly to the elements, and colour comprises an important aspect in the full meaning of the card.

The Luscher Colour Test

The Luscher Colour Test is conducted using a boxed set of cards, including instructions, that was developed in the 1900s as a psychological profiling tool by a psychologist named Luscher. The patient selects pieces of shaped cards in various colour combinations. The "reader" uses these choices to understand the character of the individual. This method has proved to be very accurate.

Aura-Soma

Aura-Soma is a colour system based on the work of Vicky Wall. It uses colours suspended in herbs, oils, and water. There are individual colours as well as dual colour combination bottles. They are luminous and beautiful. Aura-Soma can be used for insight into character, for divination, and for developing the energy field and rebalancing health states.

A Do-It-Yourself Test

Treat yourself to some cards or pieces of paper in as many colours as you can find, including black, white, gold, silver, copper, and anything else you come across. Give each piece a meaning and write it on the back. Possible meanings include: being lucky in love, being unlucky in love, being able to earn money, being able to win money, not having any money, being all right as far as money is concerned, and so on. Use ideas about health, weight gain or successful dieting, travel, parties and visits, children, babies, neighbors, pets, relatives, cars, bikes, and buses—and anything else that you can think of. Try matching the idea with the colour meanings.

Now find a willing guinea pig and get him or her to shuffle the papers around, touching all of them, and then have the individual pick three. These may be complementary colours, those that the person likes, or just those that caught his or her eye on that particular occasion. Now see what comes up.

Even if the experiment doesn't work all that well, you and your friend will have had a good giggle. The chances are that it will work, though, because so much that is unexplainable does—and at least this is a safe form of psychic experimentation.

Healing with Colour

15

Colour healing is an ancient science and art, practiced since the beginning of time. Observation of the properties of colour in nature led to the application of colour in various forms to address physical, emotional, mental, and spiritual ailments of humans and animals.

The principle of colour healing is based on the fact that each person or animal is comprised of a matrix of bodies, each functioning at a different vibrational frequency, connected and working together to support the whole organism. Each "body" of the matrix responds to different stimuli according to its structure. As one "body" is treated, there is a subsequent response and change induced within the other "bodies." For example, if you apply colour to the physical body of a person, there will be a response and subsequent change within the emotional, mental, and spiritual bodies of that individual.

Choosing Colours for Healing

Colours can be chosen by many methods and for different reasons. Each disease state has a colour that can be identified as representing it. By applying the opposite colour, you can treat the energy condition at a vibrational level. To treat an acute problem, you need to identify the colour of the problem and then apply the opposite colour.

To treat a chronic problem, you need to not only identify the colour of the problem as well as its opposite colour and then apply it, but also identify the chakra to which it relates and treat that chakra.

- To balance the emotional energy field, use only chakra colours.

- To balance the mental energy field, use Tree of Life colours (see the section "The Tree of Life—Colour on the Tree," p. 147).

The general principle is that the warm colours are stimulating, the cool colours are sedating, and green is balancing and toning.

To Affect the Blood and Organs

- Clear, dark blues are cooling and soothing.

- Grass greens are resting and invigorating.

- Orange and yellows are inspiring and illuminating.

- Bright reds to pinks are stimulating and exciting.

To Affect the Nervous System

- Shades of violet are cooling and soothing.

- Grass greens are resting and toning.

- Medium yellows and orange are inspiring, illuminating, and motivating.

- Bright reds are stimulating and exciting.

- Always finish off with a white light bath.

Red

- Use reds in small doses to kick-start the system.

- Use red for short durations to heat up cold places; red is good for anemia.

- Red works like magic for skin irritations that have the potential to leave scars, such as chicken pox or any other kind of rash.

Pink

- Pink is beneficial for skin conditions and puffiness.

- Pink comforts loneliness.

- Pink helps the person to lose weight if he or she needs to do so.

Orange

- Orange balances emotions.

- Orange awakens creativity and stimulates ambition.

- Orange eases respiratory conditions, strengthens the lungs, pancreas, and spleen, and is good for asthma and bronchitis.

- Use orange for constipation.

- Use orange for lack of vitality.

- Epilepsy may also be treated with orange-charged water daily over a long period of time.

- Apricot stimulates appetite and peach nourishes muscle tissue.

Yellow

- Yellow assists learning and aids concentration.

- Use yellow to ease indigestion and flatulence and aid elimination.

- Yellow helps ease headaches.

Green

- Green helps to balance and cleanse the system.

- Use green to ease nervous conditions.

- Green aids relaxation and awakens prosperity.

- Use green to improve vision and blood pressure.

Turquoise

- Turquoise acts as a tonic to the nervous system and stimulates activity. The tonic attributes do not manifest themselves in a hysterical manner but with calmness and awareness.

Medium Blue

- Medium blue is calming and cools the body or joints.

- Medium blue awakens artistic creativity.

- Use medium blue to ease respiration.

Dark Blue

- Dark blue accelerates healing after surgery.

- Dark blue helps heal bones when combined with green (teal blue).

- Use dark blue to open inner vision.

Purple

- Purple detoxifies the system.

- Use purple to help overcome obsessions and negativity.

- Use purple with white light.

Violet

- Violet is beneficial for skeletal problems.

- Use violet to purify and detoxify.

- Violet is deeply sedative and antiseptic, as well as deeply cooling.

- Use violet to awaken spiritual attunement.

Types of Treatment

Physical applications of colour can be carried out through dietary changes, eye-saturation exercises, drinking solarized water, as well as colour changes in clothing and the environment.

Applications of colour to the energy field that directly affect the emotional and the mental bodies are crystal healing, application of coloured lights, colour breathing, and colour projection.

Colour applied to the spiritual dimension of an individual is carried out through visualization or application within a ceremonial healing rite. For example, healing rites exist among Native Americans and Tibetan Buddhists, and in Hindu healing traditions, in which mandalas or spirit images are drawn out in coloured sand on the ground. This process is frequently carried out in conjunction with meditation, music, incense, and prayer to address problems within the various layers of the energy field of the patient.

You can perform the treatments that I list below for yourself, or you may want to consult a professional.

Dietary Changes

On a simple level, you should try to eat foods that contain all the colours of the spectrum in your diet every day. Each colour contains particular minerals, vitamins, and nourishment that your body requires.

Changing Colours in Your Clothing and Environment

Refer to the chapters "Develop Your Colour Awareness," which deals with fashion, and "Decor" and think carefully about what you can do to change the colours of your clothing and environment to support your healing process.

Eye-Saturation Exercises

Choose a colour or colours that you think contain the properties you wish to encourage, either physically or energetically. Find a paper in the appropriate colour or colours and cut out a shape. The shapes themselves have meaning:

A square encourages stability.

A circle promotes harmony and wholeness.

A triangle stimulates dynamic activity and flow.

Pin the paper up on a *white* surface so that it is at eye level when you sit at least one foot away from it. The white surface is important, as it provides the best contrast for the eye to take in the light.

Relax your body and eyes and stare at the coloured shape, keeping your eyes as steady as possible. Focus on your breathing, and in a relaxed manner, while staring at the colour, feel that as you inhale, you are drawing the colour into your eyes, and imagine that as you exhale, you are filling your body with that colour.

Eventually you will begin to see a film of another colour forming over the coloured paper; this is the astral complementary colour. When this happens or when your eyes become tired, close your eyes and watch what you see in your mind's eye. Allow the coloured image to float in the center of that space. You will see it go through the rest of the colours of the spectrum and then fade.

When it has faded, repeat the exercise two more times. At the end, rub your hands together and cup them over your open eyes, and then feel the warmth from your hands relaxing and energizing your eyes. Repeat this once a day for at least one week or until you feel that the desired effect has been achieved.

You can have some amazing results with this treatment. I once recommended that a client who had problems with lethargy, lack of social life, and lack of motivation cut out an orange triangle and do this exercise. Within one month, he found a job and sorted out his finances. He started to volunteer for an amateur theater company—something he had always wanted to do but had never had the confidence to carry out. Because he said that he was "feeling blue," I selected the colour orange; it symbolizes motivation, drive, ambition, and sociability. Interestingly, the astral complement to orange is pale turquoise, which is a colour that encourages risk taking, freedom of expression, networking, and theatrical endeavors.

Solarized Water

Two-thirds of our bodies are made up of water. We need to drink at least one to two quarts of water a day to cleanse the system.

Magnetized or charged water can assist the body with healing. Through ritual, thought, or exposure to magnets, sunlight, or channeled energy, water subtly changes its molecular structure. Charging water with specific colour frequencies is an effective way to affect the physical and subtle states. The water takes on the properties of the colour, and the individual can then swallow the water to absorb the colour energy into his or her body.

Water can also be solarized (exposed to sunlight). In this method, the sunlight energizes the water and activates it, allowing the water to absorb the colour vibrations. Dr. Edwin Babbitt, of Kilner screen fame, suggests that milk, sugar, and pulverized gum arabic can also be charged, as they are fairly neutral substances.

It is very easy to solarize water. You can use either a coloured glass container or a clear glass container wrapped in the desired colour. You can also lay the desired colour on top of the container. Choose your colours carefully. Alternatively, place a coloured stone or crystal in the water.

Place the water on a windowsill to absorb the morning sunlight for one to three hours. Once it has been fully charged, store the solarized water in the refrigerator in a clean glass container labeled with the colour and the date it was made. It will last for one week, and then you will need to make a fresh batch.

Solarized water can be drunk in small quantities, either in a dram dose or as drops in a sherry wine glass, several times a day until the problem is resolved. Alternatively, take a teaspoon of the water in the morning before eating and in the evening before going to bed, either directly or in a small amount of another liquid, such as fruit juice or milk; drink the whole glass. Continue taking the solarized water internally until the problem begins to be resolved. The water can also be used externally as a wash or compress.

Crystal Healing

Crystal healing is a huge subject in itself, so we can touch upon it only briefly in this book. Crystals work on the electromagnetic field. The clarity of the crystal and its colour influence its effect. Crystal healers apply crystals to the chakras or area of injury in order to speed recovery. Holding an appropriately coloured crystal while meditating or having one or more in your environment will exert an effect upon your energy field.

Application of Coloured Light

The application of coloured light is a specialized area, so you might wish to consult a colour healer. Coloured lights are specifically chosen to bathe a chakra or part of the body or perhaps the whole body in order to bring about changes in the energy field. Another approach may be to take an aura-light bath by sitting under a lamp with a coloured bulb. If you find it hard to obtain coloured bulbs, you can put cellophane over the lampshade so that the light shines through it—but take care that it doesn't burn. Sit under the light for fifteen minutes maximum per session. The light is absorbed through the energy field, skin, and eyes.

Colour Breathing

Colour is applied to the chakras to kick-start the process of self-healing. We can also use colour visualization and breathing techniques to send specific vibrations of life force to different parts of the body as well as the chakras. Choose colours that address your problems, visualize the colours, and then use the technique that I explain in the next section.

For example, if you suffer from "hot" arthritis, then you need to choose a colour to cool the heat of the inflammation (a blue) as well as another colour to lubricate and heal the joint and muscles around the area (peach). Often the complementary colour is applicable. Another way of looking at it might be that arthritis is a red disease (inflammatory) so a blue-green might be applied to the joints to counteract it. This would cool and harmonize the function of the joints. You need to think carefully about the symptoms you want to address. Remember that there is always a psychological aspect to take into consideration regarding both the disease as well as the colours you choose to heal it with.

If the process gets too complicated and you have trouble deciding what colour to use, the best solution is to use white light, with the mental instruction that the affected areas will pick up the colours of the spectrum as required for the healing to be initiated. You must include this instruction in your mental program. However, it would be better for you to try to figure the colours out properly rather than just fall into the habit of using white light.

Once you have chosen the colours you wish to concentrate on, work through the colours, breathing each one for about two minutes, and then finish with a minute or so of white light. Do this once a day until the problem is addressed. It is better if done before breakfast or the evening meal, not the last thing at night, as it is too stimulating.

Breathing Technique for Specific Colours

1.   Sit upright in a comfortable and relaxed position.

2. Place the tip of the tongue against the roof of the mouth just behind the front teeth.

3. Inhale slowly through the nostrils for a count of five or six.

4. Hold for a count of twelve.

5. Exhale slowly through the mouth for a count of five or six.

6. Do this several times to establish a rhythm.

7. As you inhale, see and feel the air coming in to the nostrils, visualize it as a particular colour, and send it to a particular area.

8. Do this with each colour for about two minutes.

9. Then send pure, crystalline, white light to fill your whole body for about one minute.

The session should last for at least five minutes.

General Colour-Breathing Technique

While breathing rhythmically . . .

1. Visualize individually the first three rays, red, orange, and yellow, flowing up from the Earth toward the solar plexus.

2. Then breathe the last three rays, blue, indigo, and violet, individually flowing downward from the air into the solar plexus.

3. Then visualize the green ray flowing into the solar plexus horizontally.

Charging Coloured Cloth

Another technique that can be used is to charge a piece of cloth with colour and energy to apply to a certain area and affect a person's aura. You need to think in terms of programming the energy to do the following:

- To be specific in a colour(s)

- To be specific in the particular part(s) of the body to be affected

- To be held within the cloth for a defined period of time before the energy dissipates

Cotton and silk are the best fabrics to charge with colour energy. You can energize a white cloth with a program, or you can program a cloth in the colour or colours you wish to convey to the subject.

You can charge objects by meditating and breathing. Determine beforehand what you want to happen and for how long you wish the fabric to hold the charge. Then install the program of what you want done by thinking of it while holding the cloth between your hands. Keep your left hand on the bottom and your right hand on top as you channel the colours or white light or cosmic energy through you. You must then feel it being absorbed and stored within the cloth. Continue until you intuitively know that the cloth is fully charged. Again, you can program yourself to be aware of the moment when the cloth is fully charged by telling yourself that the covering hand will float away of its own accord—owing to the wisdom of your body!

You can lay the energized fabric on the part of the body that requires help and amplify the effect by breathing rhythmically and focusing on increasing the energy flow through you. Wait until you are ready, then visualize the colour, lean forward, and bring your mouth close to the cloth. Exhale heavily and slowly upon it, then inhale again, seeing and feeling the coloured breath penetrating the body and restoring balance. Continue this for several minutes or until you are intuitively aware that the process has been completed.

Colour Projection

In colour projection, instead of using colour for self-healing, you use mental projection healing on someone else's chakra system. This process affects the emotional plane, and the ripple effect moves upward to affect the mental plane as well as downward to affect the physical one. You can use the colour-breathing techniques as explained previously, but instead of absorbing the colour yourself, you exhale through the material while projecting the colour mentally toward someone else. If the person is with you, you could extend your hand as you gaze at the body part or chakra you wish to affect, while you breathe that colour toward them. You can also work on someone at a distance by imagining that person absorbing the colour into the sick or ailing area of his or her body.

However, before you work on someone else, practice on yourself! These subtle techniques work, so consider the process carefully and be sure to ask the person's permission before doing anything.

Colour and the Esoteric Dimension

16

Colour is used in all spiritual traditions as a potent expression of sacred energies. One touches the divine when one puts oneself "in the Light," but this is too large a subject to address in a book of this kind.

Take a moment to reflect upon any spiritual ritual you have engaged in. Every festival has colour associations that work their magic upon you. For instance, we use reds, greens, and gold for Christmas, blue and silver for Hannukah, purple and yellow for Easter, orange and black for Halloween, and so on. By using colour associated with your spiritual tradition, you will automatically be more in touch with your own spiritual dimension.

This book is called *Colour Therapy Plain and Simple*, so it is not the place for a deep explanation of all the various esoteric traditions, but you might like just a tiny glimpse at the colours and some of the associated ideas within each system. This chapter will provide a quick overview of traditions that use colour: the Kabala, the Seven Rays, astrology and crystal correspondences.

The Tree of Life

The Tree of Life design of the Kabala is divided into two main parts, separated by what is known as the "Abyss." The three Sephirah, or centers, above the Abyss relate to the triple Godhead, and the seven Sephirah below, to Creation. In light and colour terms, the three Sephirah above relate to the principle of light and to its presence or absence, denoted by white and black. Immediately below the Abyss we have the three primary colours of blue, red, and yellow, followed by the secondary colours of green, orange, and purple, or violet. The final Sephirah represents all the variations of colour found in nature.

The Tree of Life—Colour on the Tree

Kether: Pure brilliance

Binah: Black

'Hokma: White

Daath: Lavender

The Abyss

Geburah: Red

'Hesed: Blue

Tiphareth: Yellow

Hod: Orange

Netzach: Green

Yesod: Purple or violet

Malkuth: Citrine, olive, black, russet

Note: "Sephirah" is Hebrew for "book." The plural is "Sephirot."

The Seven Rays

The Hindus speak of the "Seven Praj patis" (Lords of Creation); the Zoroastrians, of the "Seven Amesha Spentas" (Immortal Holy Ones). In Egypt the rays were termed the "Seven Mystery Gods."

The Jews call them the "Seven Sephirot" (Holy Books). In the Christian Bible they are referred to as the "Seven Spirits Before the Throne of God." In the Theosophical concept, the term "Seven Planetary Chain Logoi" is generally used.

The Principles Associated with the Rays

Ray 1: Will plus power

Ray 2: Love plus wisdom

Ray 3: Active intelligence

Ray 4: Harmony through conflict

Ray 5: Concrete knowledge

Ray 6: Devotion plus idealism

Ray 7: Ceremonial order

The seven rays are the embodiments of seven types of force that bring into being the seven qualities of deity (seven aspects of God). One idea that was popular in medieval times was that of the heavenly "Music of the Spheres"; we can see this expressed in colour every time we see a rainbow.

Ray 1

- Will plus power
- The spirit
- Life
- Ideas

- The mental body

- Purpose (in life)

Ray colour: Red

Human principle: Life vitality

Divine principle: The one life, spirit

Concerned with: Force, energy, action

The first ray is that of will plus power, for will becomes power when it is applied. This ray is concerned with both the creation and the destruction of life.

The red colour that is associated with this ray is an activating, energizing colour that is related to the element of fire.

Ray 2

- Love plus wisdom

- The soul

- Consciousness

- Ideals

- Astral body

- Quality (of life)

Ray colour: Light blue

Human principle: The aura

Divine principle: Love

Concerned with: Consciousness, expansion, initiation

This second ray, love plus wisdom, is concerned with the "under-standing of God" and with the expression of ideals. This is not something that is related to rational thought processes, so the second ray governs intuition that leads to knowledge. One of the special virtues of those upon this ray is the love of truth.

The colour blue associated with this ray is a calming, sooth-ing colour, and people with a blue aura often exhibit many of the virtues mentioned above.

Ray 3

- Active intelligence
- The personality
- Appearance
- Images
- Physical body (form of life)

Ray colour: Green

Human principle: Lower mind

Divine principle: Universal mind

Concerned with: Adaptation, development, evolution

In Kabala, the colours attributed to the Sephirot are based upon physical colour mixing. The seven rays, though, are concerned with light, and when mixing light, the three primary colours are red, blue, and green.

Ray 4

- Harmony through conflict
- The human kingdom
- The intuitive plane

Ray colour: Yellow

Human principle: Understanding, vision, spiritual perception

Divine principle: Intuition

Element: Fire

The fourth ray is known as the ray of harmony through conflict or the ray of struggle. It is the main ray of humankind at the present time. This is the ray through which self-control is obtained. Here we have the alliance of the first ray, will plus power, and the second, love plus wisdom, so it is concerned with the balancing of opposites.

Ray 5

- Concrete knowledge
- The animal kingdom
- The lower mental plane
- Mentality

Ray colour: Indigo

Human principle: The intellect

Divine principle: Higher knowledge

Element: Air

The fifth ray is the ray of science. It is called "concrete knowledge," and it is related to the lower mind. It is associated with research, specialization, and technical correctness. Here we see the energies of the first ray, will plus power, being directed toward the discovery of knowledge, especially of the form of things.

Ray 6

- Devotion
- The vegetable kingdom
- The astral plane

Ray colour: Silvery rose

Human principle: Desire

Divine principle: Devotion plus idealism

Element: Water

Although this ray is said to be a mix of the second ray, love plus wisdom, and the third ray, active intelligence, many of its qualities seem more appropriate to the first ray, will plus power. In seeking to create a perfect world, there is also a requirement to destroy the things that do not conform to those ideals.

Ray 7

- Ceremonial order
- The mineral kingdom
- The physical and etheric plane

Ray colour: Violet

Human principle: Etheric force or prana

Divine principle: Energy

Element: Earth

This ray is called "ceremonial order," and it is said to be coming into force at this time as part of the dawning of the Age of Aquarius. At one level it is the ray that makes someone delight in doing things properly. It is the ray of the high priest, the court chamberlain, and the orthodox doctor, or anyone who is concerned with the proper form of things. As with all the other rays, it has both positive and negative manifestations.

Astrology and Crystal Correspondences

The question of the relationship between colour and the planets and signs of the zodiac, in addition to the crystals that are associated with astrology, is problematic. There are as many ideas as to what these relationships should be as there are authors on the subject, particularly in reference to the zodiac signs. Crystals are composed of various chemical combinations that produce colour. When used in healing, crystals amplify the qualities of these colours and influence the energy field of the individual.

In these examples of colours, crystals, and astrology, we see how the three primary colours give rise to the secondary colours and intermediate ones to form a total of twelve, beginning with red, which is the usual attribution for Aries.

Here are some examples taken from a range of sources:

Aries (March 21–April 20)

Concepts: Adventure, impulsiveness, fresh starts

Colours: Red, carmine red, brilliant red, pinks, black, purple

Crystals: Ruby, red jasper, diamond, bloodstone, garnet, ruby, aventurine, fire agate, Brazilian agate, bloodstone hematite, iron

Taurus (April 21–May 21)

Concepts: Concern with resources, comfort, safety, property, money

Colours: Blue, pink, brown, green, red-orange, yellow, cream, tan

Crystals: Emerald, rose quartz, sapphire, turquoise, jade, lapis lazuli, selenite, chrysocolla, copper

Gemini (May 22–June 21)

Concepts: Communication, education, travel, language

Colours: Violet, varicoloured, orange, yellows, crystal blue, check patterns

Crystals: Citrine, agate, chrysoprase, pearl, agate, aventurine, rutilated quartz, aquamarine, blue sapphire, apopholite, celestite, sandstone, cinnabar, mercury

Cancer (June 22–July 22)

Concepts: Love of home and family, moodiness

Colours: Silver, white, soft shades, orange-yellow, green, blue-green, grays, tans, milky cream

Crystals: Moonstone, mother-of-pearl, pearls, calcite, opal, fire opal, peacock ore, silver

Leo (July 23–August 23)

Concepts: Creativity, charisma

Colours: Gold, orange, yellow, bright red, bright colours, royal colours

Crystals: Tiger-eye, diamond, zircon, onyx, tourmaline, amber, carnelian, yellow topaz, petrified wood, rhodochrosite, gold

Virgo (August 24–September 22)

Concepts: Practicality, fussiness, good craftsmanship

Colours: Gray, navy, spotted, yellow-green, violet, blue, green, brown, yellow

Crystals: Carnelian, sapphire, jasper, jade, agate, watermelon tourmaline amazonite, peridot, moss agate, geode, cinnabar, mercury

Libra (September 23–October 23)

Concepts: Organization, negotiations and mediation, good taste

Colours: Rose, blue, pink, pastel shades, green, yellow, crimson, white

Crystals: Aventurine, lapis lazuli, opal, chrysoprase, green tourmaline, lepidolite, ametrine, apopholite, bloodstone, citrine, kyanite, nephrite, opal, fire opal, white opal, copper

Scorpio (October 24–November 22)

Concepts: Moodiness, intensity and depth, secretiveness, healing ability

Colours: Greenish blue, wine red, brown, black, purples

Crystals: Citrine, beryl, tourmalated quartz, moldavite, labradorite, malachite, moonstone, iron, plutonium

Sagittarius (November 23 – December 21)

Concepts: Jack-of-all-trades, humor, travel

Colours: Purple, blue, yellow, red, gold, orange reds, bright colours

Crystals: Sodalite, amethyst, topaz, sapphire, lapis lazuli, sugilite, sodalite, azurite, chlorite, Herkimer diamond, labradorite, fire opal, peridot, turquoise, tin

Capricorn (December 22–January 20)

Concepts: Deferred gratification, steady climber, seriousness

Colours: Black, dark shades, blue-violet, indigo, gray, browns, deep colours

Crystals: Obsidian, garnet, diamond, tiger-eye, malachite, fluorite, black tourmaline, green tourmaline, smoky quartz, trilobite, lead

Aquarius (January 21–February 19)

Concepts: Unusual approach to life, one who is in his or her own world, teachers

Colours: Electric blue, lilac, violet, indigo, azure, multicolour, neon, unusual shades

Crystals: Amethyst, clear quartz, garnet, aquamarine, hematite, amber, lead

Pisces (February 20–March 20)

Concepts: Artistry and impracticality, changeability, psychic

Colours: Sea green, red-violet, blue, green, white, pastels

Crystals: Clear quartz, bloodstone, sugilite, iolite, amethyst, opal, coral, blue lace agate, fire opal, tin

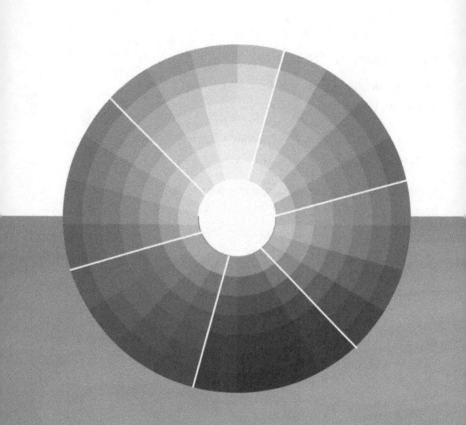

The
Science
of Colour

17

This chapter is for those of you who want to understand colour from a scientific perspective.

Light is life. All life on our planet is nourished and maintained by the light it needs to absorb in order to exist. From a spiritual perspective, the Sun represents God or the source of life. From a scientific viewpoint, light is electromagnetic energy produced by the Sun. These waves are vibrations of electric and magnetic fields that pass through space. Light travels in darkness but is not perceived until it bounces off something. This is why space is seen as dark, until an object that reflects light is present. Everything that we see is reflected light. When light waves bounce off objects and into our eyes, they create a sensation of light that is perceived by the brain as a particular frequency or what we term colour; for example, a high frequency is perceived as blue and a low frequency as red.

The corresponding molecular structure and subsequent colour of an object cause light rays to be mixed, absorbed, and reflected in varying speeds and intensities. Objects that appear to be dark absorb more light rays and therefore reflect less light back to the eyes, creating an illusion of a dark colour. Conversely, lighter objects reflect more light, giving the illusion of more brightness and intensity. For example, when light strikes a red surface, that surface absorbs all the other rays and reflects back the red wavelengths. This is how we see that the object is red.

What Is Colour?

Colour is a property of light. Light travels in waves—electromagnetic waves. These waves are vibrations of electric and magnetic fields that pass through space. In physics, the visible spectrum has three primary colours, which are red, green, and blue. Chemically, colour is derived from pigments and compounds, and the three primary colours in this environment are red, yellow, and blue. The combination of any two of these colours will give a third colour—a secondary colour.

Colour is simply light of different wavelengths and frequencies, and light is just one form of energy, made up of photons. The visible spectrum as we see it consists of the rainbow.

Our retinas have three types of colour receptors in the form of cones. We can detect only three of the colours in the spectrum, red, blue, and green. These colours are called additive primaries. These three colours combine to create all the other colours we see. The seven colours of the spectrum all have varying wavelengths and frequencies. Red is at the lower end of the spectrum and has a higher wavelength but lower frequency than does violet, which is at the top end of the spectrum. Violet has a lower wavelength and higher frequency. Just outside the normally visible spectrum are infrared and ultraviolet, though some people can at least partially see these wavelengths as well.

The seven colours of the rainbow become visible when a prism is placed in the path of sunlight. As the light passes through the prism, it is split by refraction into the seven visible colours of the spectrum. The amount of energy in a given light wave is proportionally related to its frequency; thus, a high-frequency light wave has a higher energy than a low-frequency light wave does. Refraction is caused by the change in speed experienced by a wave of light when it changes medium. Higher-frequency colours are violet, indigo, and blue. Lower-frequency colours are yellow, orange, and red.

Sir Isaac Newton proved that light was made up of the seven colours of the spectrum. This spectrum of light can be recreated in the home by using three flashlights. This is called colour by addition.

Cover the front of one flashlight with a blue light filter, the second with a green light filter, and the third with a red light filter. Shine the flashlights on a white wall or surface. The effect is best achieved in a very dark room with a white wall. Arrange the lights so that the beams of light just overlap one another. The result is that in the middle of the three light beams, the area is white. Where each of the colours overlap, magenta, cyan (a pale turquoise or duck-egg greenish blue), and yellow are produced.

Combinations of other colours—blue with yellow, or red with cyan—can also make white light. Bringing all three light beams together produces just white light.

The colour of the surface on which you shine the lights makes a big difference in the colours that are (or are not) produced. A white wall will display the colours as in the diagram, but a yellow, red, or blue wall will produce very different results.

- A *red* wall will absorb the green and blue light and emit red light.

- A *green* wall will absorb the red and blue light and emit green light.

- A *blue* wall will absorb the red and green light and emit blue light.

Physical Properties of Colour

Each colour of the spectrum has its own properties in the form of its wavelength and frequency. Although white could be said to be a colour, it is not included in the spectrum as it is in fact made up of all the colours of the spectrum. Sir Isaac Newton proved this by passing sunlight through a glass prism, which produced a rainbow spectrum on a surface. He then proceeded to use a second glass prism and combined the two rainbows. This combination produced white light.

Colour Properties

Colour	Wavelength in Nanometers	Frequency in THz	Related Chakra
Violet	380-400	750	Crown
Indigo	400-450	700	Brow
Blue	450-595	600	Throat
Green	495-578	550	Heart
Yellow	570-590	500	Solar plexus
Orange	590-620	480	Sacral
Red	620-770	430	Base/root

How We See Colour

Our eyes contain light-sensitive receptors called rods and cones. There are about 120 million rods and about 6 to 7 million cones in the human eye. The rods are more than one thousand times as sensitive as the cones, but they are not sensitive to colour; they perceive images as black, white, and different shades of gray. The rods respond better to blue but very little to red. Each cone contains one of three pigments, which are sensitive to red, green, or blue.

People who suffer from colour blindness have fewer of some cones than normal so they get some colours confused. If we lose our eyesight entirely, the body adapts and receives colour rays through the skin. It takes time for a person who has lost his or her eyesight to adapt, because he or she will have to sense the energy difference in the colours rather than "see" the colours.

Everything we see is reflected light. When light waves bounce off objects and into our eyes, they create a sensation of light that is perceived by the brain as a particular frequency or what we term "colour"; for example, a high frequency is perceived as blue and a low frequency as red. The corresponding molecular structure and subsequent pigmentation of an object cause light rays to be mixed, absorbed, and reflected in varying speeds and intensities. Objects that appear to be dark absorb more light rays and therefore reflect less light back to the eyes, creating an illusion of a dark colour. Conversely, lighter objects reflect more light, giving the illusion of more brightness and intensity.

Primary, Secondary, and Tertiary Colours

Primary Colours

Primary colours cannot be produced through the mixing of other colours. There are three types of primary colours:

- **Additive primaries:** Red, blue, and green

- **Subtractive primaries:** Red, blue, and yellow

- **Process colours:** Cyan, magenta, and yellow (plus black)

Additive colours are produced by radiant sources, such as the Sun. When the three additive primaries are mixed together, they produce white. These are the colours you see on your computer—the colours are generated through light. Each additive primary represents almost a third of the spectrum; thus, when you add another primary, more of the spectrum is present. When all three primaries are added, almost the entire spectrum is present in the form of white light. Mixing these primaries in varying amounts can produce a large section of the visible spectrum. They are used in theatrical lighting, videos, film recorders, and television and computer monitors.

Subtractive primary colours produce pigments, and these relate to the colours we see in physical objects. They are called subtractive because the colour that we see depends upon the frequencies within white light that are absorbed by an object and those that are reflected.

Process colours are those used in printing processes and inkjet printers. These colours are basically subtractive primary colours since they are physical pigments. The addition of black allows for a wide range of hues.

Secondary Colours

Secondary colours are produced when any two of the primary colours are mixed.

The *additive primaries* create secondary colours as follows:

Red + Blue = Magenta

Blue + Green = Cyan

Green + Red = Yellow

The *subtractive primaries* create secondary colours:

Red + Blue = Violet

Blue + Yellow = Green

Yellow + Red = Orange

The *process primaries* create secondary colours as follows:

Cyan + Magenta = Blue

Magenta + Yellow = Red

Yellow + Cyan = Green

Tertiary Colours

Tertiary colours are a mixture of any two secondary colours. The combinations fall into two categories:

Complementary colours, which are colours that are placed opposite each other on the colour wheel; or

Analogous colours, which are colours that are placed next to each other on the colour wheel.

Even light rays that are beyond the visible spectrum are useful. Infrared lamps keep foods hot and can help damaged muscles to heal. Exposure to ultraviolet light helps cure jaundice and psoriasis.

As we have seen, colour is energy—being light of varying wavelengths. Light is fundamental for life, whether human, animal, or plant. Light has a profound effect on our brain, influencing the activity of the pineal gland, which appears to be a regulatory force for the release of several neurotransmitters, sending messages within the brain as well as messages that prompt hormone release.

Light is not only part of the electromagnetic spectrum; it is an important part of the universal spectrum of vibrations or frequencies that includes sound at its lower end. If we take the frequency of any specific musical note and double this frequency enough times, we will eventually reach the light spectrum. The only difference between the seven colours of the light spectrum and the seven notes of the sound spectrum is the rate of vibration. This also corresponds to the seven energy chakras. It seems that the human body itself is a manifestation of the universal harmonic chord.

The pyramid diagram is another way of viewing the colour spectrum and shows the seven rainbow colours in order of their frequency.

Pyramid Diagram

Colour Wheels

A common way of showing the relationships among different colours is through the use of colour wheels, two diagrams of which are given here. One is for additive colours and the other for subtractive colours. As stated earlier, it is always important to remember which type you are dealing with so as not to create confusion regarding the relationships among primary, secondary, and complementary colours.

Colour Wheel and Mixing Colours

When we think of the primary colours (**1**), we immediately visualize bright, saturated colours such as fire-engine red, pumpkin orange, sunflower yellow, emerald green, and so on. This is true of all the bright or saturated colours from which all hues are formed. However, the primary colours are the three colours that cannot be sourced from elsewhere. In physical terms, these are red, yellow, and blue.

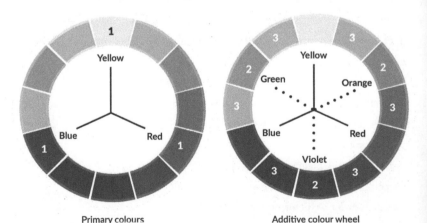

Primary colours   Additive colour wheel

By mixing two primary colours together, we get what are termed the secondary colours (**2**): orange (red plus yellow), green (yellow plus blue), and violet (red plus blue). The tertiary colours (**3**) result from the combination of secondary colours:

- Green + purple = olive
- Orange + purple = russet
- Green + orange = citrine

We can also call colours hot or cold based on the physical and psychological effects that they exert on us. The hot colours are reds, oranges, and yellows, and they have a stimulating and activating effect on the system. The cool colours are blues, greens, and violets; they have a calming and even anesthetizing effect.

Opposite or complementary colours balance each other out. This actually happens physically. If you stare at a red surface for a minute, then move your eyes to a white surface, you will see an afterimage of pale green. Our eyes must physically complete the whole spectrum after each intense exposure to light. This is why when a flashbulb temporarily blinds you, the afterimage goes from white to black and then from the cool to the hot end of the spectrum before it completely fades. These principles are used in colour-healing techniques.

Acknowledgments

I would like to thank my husband, Douglas, for his patience and unstinting support and his work on Kabala and the Seven Rays, subjects that appear in chapter 16, "Colour and the Esoteric Dimension." I pay tribute to some of the many teachers along the path that contributed to my being able to write this book. These include Dr. Robert Massey and Christopher Hills of the University of the Trees, Marilyn Rossner of the Spiritual Science Fellowship, Swami Vishnu Devananda, Swami Rudi, and Gerry and Nancy Hillman. My heartfelt thanks also go out to the skills of Cindy Hurn, who helped me with my writing struggles, as well as to all my friends and colleagues whose belief and support during this process have encouraged me enormously.

Try another practical guide in the
ORION PLAIN AND SIMPLE series

ORION PLAIN AND SIMPLE

astrology
CASS & JANIE JACKSON

ORION PLAIN AND SIMPLE

totem animals
CELIA M GUNN

ORION PLAIN AND SIMPLE

runes
KIM FARNELL

ORION PLAIN AND SIMPLE

palmistry
SASHA FENTON

ORION PLAIN AND SIMPLE

body reading
SASHA FENTON

ORION PLAIN AND SIMPLE

numerology
ANNE CHRISTIE

ORION PLAIN AND SIMPLE

chinese astrology
JONATHAN DEE

ORION PLAIN AND SIMPLE

crystals
CASS & JANIE JACKSON

ORION PLAIN AND SIMPLE

reincarnation
KRYS & JASS GODLY

ORION PLAIN AND SIMPLE

angels
BELETA GREENAWAY

ORION PLAIN AND SIMPLE

wicca
LEANNA GREENAWAY

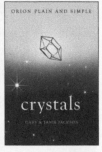

ORION PLAIN AND SIMPLE

herbs
MARLENE HOUGHTON

ORION PLAIN AND SIMPLE

i ching
KIM FARNELL

ORION PLAIN AND SIMPLE

flower essences
LINDA PERRY

OG